GW00357277

How to Stop Smoking Without Gaining Weight

BOOKS BY MARTIN KATAHN, PhD

The Rotation Diet Cookbook
(with Terri Katahn)

The T-Factor Diet

The T-Factor Fat Gram Counter
(with Jamie Pope-Cordle)

One Meal at a Time

The Low-Fat Fast Food Guide
(with Jamie Pope-Cordle)

The 200 Calorie Solution

Beyond Diet

The Rotation Diet

The Low-Fat Good Food Cookbook
(with Terri Katahn)

How to Stop Smoking Without Gaining Weight

MARTIN KATAHN, PhD

BANTAM BOOKS
LONDON · NEW YORK · TORONTO · SYDNEY · AUCKLAND

HOW TO STOP SMOKING
WITHOUT GAINING WEIGHT

A BANTAM BOOK : 0 553 40948 4

First publication in Great Britain

PRINTING HISTORY
Bantam edition published 1995

Copyright © Katahn Associates, Inc. 1994

The right of Martin Katahn to be identified as the author of this work has been asserted in accordance with sections 77 and 78 of the Copyright Designs and Patents Act 1988.

Conditions of Sale
1. This book is sold subject to the condition that it shall not, by way of trade or otherwise, be lent, re-sold, hired out or otherwise circulated in any form of binding or cover other than that in which it is published and without a similar condition including this condition being imposed on the subsequent purchaser.
2. This book is sold subject to the Standard Conditions of Sale of Net Books and may not be re-sold in the UK below the net price fixed by the publishers for the book.

Set in Linotype Palatino and Helvetica Narrow by
Phoenix Typesetting, Ilkley, West Yorkshire.

Bantam Books are published by Transworld Publishers Ltd,
61–63 Uxbridge Road, Ealing, London W5 5SA,
in Australia by Transworld Publishers (Australia) Pty Ltd,
15–25 Helles Avenue, Moorebank, NSW 2170,
and in New Zealand by Transworld Publishers (NZ) Ltd,
3 William Pickering Drive, Albany, Auckland.

Reproduced, printed and bound in Great Britain by
Cox & Wyman Ltd, Reading, Berks.

How to Stop Smoking Without Gaining Weight

Contents

Acknowledgements

I'd like to extend special thanks to Jacqueline Goffaux, PhD, of the Institute for Smoking Prevention and Cessation at the Dayani Human Performance Center of Vanderbilt University, for her help in reviewing my manuscript for scientific accuracy. Any errors that remain are, of course, my own responsibility.

Thanks to Marlene Otto, MA, RD, for helping to compile the Fat and Carbohydrate Counter in Appendix C.

And, once again, many thanks to my agent, Richard Pine, and the team at W.W. Norton & Company, that helped me put this book together; my editor, Starling Lawrence; manuscript editor, Debra Makay; production manager, Andy Marasia; editorial assistant, Patricia Chui; and Managing editor, Nancy Palmquist.

A Note on Measures for the British Edition

Since *How to Stop Smoking Without Gaining Weight* originated in the USA some of the measurements for servings are given by volume using the American cup. Measurement by volume is often the most sensible way, for a serving of vegetables or cooked rice, for example, and to give an idea of the appropriate quantity of fruit. To be accurate, measure a 'cup' up to the 8-fluid-ounce (225-ml) mark in a standard measuring jug; you will soon be able to judge the proper amounts. As a rough guide, 3 stalks of raw celery (sliced), 2 medium carrots (sliced) or 3 ounces (80 g) of raw sliced mushrooms all approximate 1 cup. Again as a rough guide, 1 piece of fruit – a small apple or orange, half a large banana, 3 ounces (80 g) of grapes (about 20), a small slice of melon or two thin (½-inch/1-cm) slices of pineapple each approximates half a cup. A normal serving of any cooked vegetable approximates one cup; a small serving or 3 rounded tablespoons half a cup. Men are often allowed vegetable servings half as big again. These approximate the 'average' and 'small' helpings that a man could expect in a restaurant or at home. Accurately the greens or marrow would come up to the 12-fluid-ounce (330-ml) level in your measuring jug (for 1½ cups), the peas or carrots to the 6-fluid-ounce (180-ml) level (for ¾ cup).

Rice and pasta such as macaroni will roughly double in volume on cooking; for porridge, use the volume of water that you require and add the appropriate quantities of oatmeal or rolled oats according to the instructions for your usual brand – i.e. for one cup of porridge use 8 fluid ounces (225-ml) of water and 3 to 4 level tablespoons of rolled oats.

In the menus and recipes most of the American cup measurements have been converted to British Imperial and metric weights on the scales given overleaf, the criterion being in each case: which is the easiest measurement to use? But in the Fat and Carbohydrate Counter in Appendix C the cup measurement has been retained more often. Spoonfuls are always level unless 'rounded' or 'heaped' is specified; and please remember that all teaspoons, including ½ and ¼ teaspoon, should be scant measures – just a little less than level.

Weights		Volume/Liquids	
1 kg	= 2 lbs 3 oz	1 litre =	1¾ pints/35 fluid oz
450 g	= 1 lb	700 ml =	1¼ pints/24 fluid oz
350 g	= 12 oz		(3 American cups)
275 g	= 10 oz	570 ml =	1 pint/20 fluid oz
225 g	= 8 oz	450 ml =	16 fluid oz
175 g	= 6 oz		(2 American cups)
145 g	= 5 oz	330 ml =	12 fluid oz
110 g	= 4 oz		(1½ American cups)
80 g	= 3 oz	225 ml =	8 fluid oz
56 g	= 2 oz		(1 American cup)
40 g	= 1½ oz	180 ml =	6 fluid oz
28 g	= 1 oz		(¾ American cup)
		110 ml =	4 fluid oz
			(½ American cup)
		25 ml =	1 fluid oz
		15 ml =	1 tablespoon
		10 ml =	1 dessertspoon
		5 ml =	1 teaspoon

Introduction

Have you been thinking that it's time to stop smoking but keep putting it off because you're worried about gaining weight?

Or are you one of those people who has already stopped smoking cigarettes, gained weight, and found yourself graduated to a whole new wardrobe a size or two larger than before?

How to Stop Smoking Without Gaining Weight will help you stop smoking without gaining an ounce, and it will help you lose whatever weight you have gained if you have already stopped. It is based on my fifteen years of professional experience as director of the Vanderbilt

Weight Management Program, my own personal experience as a former pack-a-day cigarette smoker, and the most recent research on smoking cessation.

To begin with, your fears about gaining weight when you stop smoking are well founded. About 70 per cent of the people who stop gain weight. Among these, the average gain is between 10 and 12 pounds (4½ – 5½ k). About one in seven women and one in ten men will gain 2 stone (14 k) or more. Some people gain at the rate of a pound (450 g) a week, or even faster. I have worked with people who ended up 3½ stone (23 k) heavier less than a year after giving up.

But don't be discouraged by these statistics! I'm certain that the advice on weight management in this book will work for you.

If you are still smoking cigarettes, you are likely to be thinking seriously about stopping or you would not be reading this book. You may be concerned about the risk of lung cancer, emphysema and heart disease, and, if you are a parent with children at home, the danger of passive smoke to their health. To stop smoking is about the very best thing you can do for your own health as well as for the health of the people around you.

Wouldn't it be a lot easier to stop and never be tempted to start again if you didn't have to worry about gaining weight? Although gaining a small amount of weight is not nearly as dangerous as smoking, the more you gain, the more you restore the risk of heart disease and certain forms of cancer that you reduced by stopping. Of course, adding more than a few pounds can result in a cosmetic disaster and a loss of self-esteem.

What's even worse about gaining weight after you stop smoking (and I really hate to say this since it is so important to stop) is that IT IS MUCH HARDER TO

LOSE A SIGNIFICANT AMOUNT OF WEIGHT THAN IT IS TO GIVE UP SMOKING! About half the adults in this country who once smoked cigarettes have, usually after several attempts, been able to stop smoking permanently. Fewer than one in ten over-weight people are able to lose a significant amount of weight and keep it off for good, no matter how many times they try.[1]

WHY I DECIDED TO WRITE A BOOK ON HOW TO STOP SMOKING WITHOUT GAINING WEIGHT

I decided that a book on how to stop smoking without gaining weight might be of value to a great many smok-ers and ex-smokers when, one day in October 1993, my wife came home after shopping for a gown to wear while performing as a concert pianist. She told me that the two salespersons who helped her at the dress shop had recently stopped smoking. One of the women had gained 12 pounds (5½ k) and was a whole dress size larger. The other woman had gained 6 pounds (2¾ k), and was on the verge of bursting her seams. They were not very happy about this and they both pleaded, 'Your husband needs to write a book on how to quit smoking without gaining weight!'

By a strange coincidence, the very day that my wife came home with this request I received a letter from a man who had gained weight after stopping smoking. Then he discovered *The T-Factor Diet* and with its help

---

[1] 'Overweight' is usually defined as being 20 per cent over the weight specified as desirable in standard weight charts.

he lost all the weight he had gained, plus an additional 2¼ stone (14½ k) that he had needed to lose before he stopped. Here is an excerpt from that letter, dated 12 October 1993:

> I am writing to say a hearty 'thank you' for your book, *The T-Factor Diet*. I found it in September 1991, after gaining ten pounds as a result of smoking cessation. Or, should I say my lack of control during that six-week period after quitting.[2] I am walking testimony to the ongoing success of your program. From September 1991 until May 1992, I lost forty-two pounds. At this writing, my weight remains at the May 1992 level, with very minor fluctuations. My range is now from 149 to 151 [about 10½ stone/68 k].

My wife's experience at the dress shop, and the receipt of this letter, encouraged me to do some research in the field of smoking cessation. I had been asked in my lectures on weight management to give advice on how to stop smoking without gaining weight many times before, but had never responded by writing a book, or even an article, about it. Aren't people already given the information they need about the many factors that lead to weight gain when they stop smoking? Isn't the best information on how to prevent weight gain easily available from the major health organizations interested in helping people to give up?

The answer is NO!

When I studied the manuals of the various agencies

---

[2] As you will discover when you understand the reasons for gaining weight when you stop smoking, this man had no need to blame a lack of control.

I discovered that, in their eagerness to get you to stop smoking, they downplay both the likelihood of gaining weight when you stop and the amount that you are likely to gain. They also do not give a full explanation of the physiological and biochemical changes that may occur in your body when you withdraw from nicotine, *changes which are out of your control.* Furthermore, the advice on how to deal with these physiological changes and prevent gaining weight after you have stopped smoking does not work for the great majority of those who stop, who end up gaining 10, 12 or even 50 pounds (4½, 5½ or even 55 k). The net result is that most quitters feel lousy about the weight they gain. And because they have been led to believe that gaining weight was going to be a minor problem or should not be happening in the first place, they feel guilty over their inability to prevent it.

In addition to studying the various smoking cessation pamphlets published by the major health organizations, I did a computer-assisted search and found over 1100 articles in the scientific literature on the biochemical effects of nicotine, metabolism, smoking cessation strategies and the problem of weight gain, written within the past ten years. When I studied these articles, I discovered a number of factors that are specific to smokers and which cause smokers in particular to gain weight when they stop. These factors are not discussed in smoking cessation manuals or, to my knowledge, in any books on weight management, including my own earlier books, *The T-Factor Diet* and *One Meal at a Time.*

That's why I decided to write this book.

In *How to Stop Smoking Without Gaining Weight* I present two closely related programmes.

The 7 + 7 Programme is designed for people who are about to stop. In this I will show you, in two consecutive seven-day training periods, how to make sure, *in advance*, that you will not gain any weight when you give up smoking, and then how to choose the best way to do it.

For people who have already stopped and who, unfortunately, may have gained some weight, I present the Ex-Smoker's Weight-Management Programme. This programme will show you what you need to do to lose weight without endangering your ability to remain a non-smoker.

So, without further introduction, let's jump in and see where you stand and what you need to do to stop smoking without gaining weight.

1
What Do You Need To Know?
What Do You Need To Do?

Do you know why most smokers gain weight when they stop?

If you are about to stop, do you know what to do to fight successfully against the craving for a cigarette the moment it hits you?

Do you know your underlying reasons for smoking, and how to deal with them so that when you stop you won't keep yearning for cigarettes?

Here are a couple of quizzes to test your understanding of the problems that are reflected in the above questions, together with a brief explanation to go with the answers. In the chapters that follow, I will go into greater detail in order to give you the weapons you will need to become a non-smoker at the weight you'd like to be.

QUIZ 1 · WHY DO YOU GAIN WEIGHT WHEN YOU STOP SMOKING?

1. TRUE OR FALSE: When you stop smoking it's possible to gain weight even though you don't consume a single calorie more than you did as a smoker.

2. TRUE OR FALSE: There is a physiological basis to the increase in appetite that most people experience when they stop smoking, and it usually does lead them to eat more than they did before.

3. TRUE OR FALSE: There is a physiological basis to the craving for sweets that develops in many people who stop smoking.

4. TRUE OR FALSE: When smokers stop, their bodies may begin to convert more of the fat in their diets to body fat than when they were smokers.

5. TRUE OR FALSE: Smoking can increase your metabolic rate so that pack-a-day smokers may be able to eat as much as 200 calories more each day without gaining weight, compared with non-smokers.

Did you answer 'true' to all the above questions? If you did, you are absolutely correct: you can gain weight when you stop smoking even if you don't eat a single calorie more than you did as a smoker. But, just to compound the problem, your appetite is also likely to increase, especially your appetite for sweets. In addition, when you withdraw from nicotine, your fat cells may start to suck up fat from your bloodstream after you have eaten at a faster rate than they did when you smoked. Finally, if you smoke about a pack of cigarettes a day and then stop, your total daily energy needs may decline by as much as 200 calories. When you add the increased rate of fat storage to the decline in your energy requirements, it means that unless you do something to compensate for these changes, you may need to consume about 300 calories less each day just to maintain your present weight when you stop smoking.[1] And all at a time when your appetite may be going berserk![2]

I will give you a full explanation of how and why these things occur in the next chapter, 'Know your Enemy'. Then, whether you are about to stop or have

---

[1] When they discuss the impact of smoking on your energy needs some experts prefer to use the term 'total daily energy expenditure' rather than 'metabolic rate', which usually refers to the rate at which your body burns calories at rest. The reason for this is, in part, that smoking may increase energy needs during physical activity even more than when you are at rest.

[2] There are a few studies in respected, peer-reviewed scientific journals that present evidence for each of these physiological changes in response to smoking cessation. If you are likely to gain a small amount of weight when you quit, it's virtually certain that at least one of these mechanisms will be operating. If you are a heavy smoker and have any genetic tendency to obesity, it's likely that several of these factors will combine to foster a large weight gain. Since it's impossible to predict which factors may operate in any particular case, an ounce of prevention is worth a pound of cure: you should be prepared to deal with all of them, *before you stop smoking*.

stopped already and gained some weight, you will understand why you must take the steps I recommend, and you will be more motivated to take them.

Now, about the smoking habit itself.

The next few paragraphs are intended primarily for smokers about to stop. However, if you have recently stopped, you should still read them and answer the questions in the quiz just in case you are continuing to struggle with the urge to smoke.

If you are still smoking cigarettes and are seriously considering giving up, you have to ask yourself:

AM I REALLY READY TO KICK THE SMOKING HABIT? AM I CONFIDENT I CAN DO IT SUCCESS-FULLY?

Two conditions are absolutely essential to be a successful quitter:

1. You must be highly motivated to stop.
2. You must be confident in your ability to do it.

It's possible to be motivated to stop, but to waver for a couple of reasons. Because stopping can be rather uncomfortable, and cigarettes have been fulfilling an important function in your life, it's natural to debate the pros and cons of giving them up. And since most people who try to stop fail in any given attempt and need to try several times before they are successful, it's natural to lack absolute confidence in your ability to succeed, especially if you have failed one or more times in the past. Thus, a lack of confidence can actually undermine your motivation.

In case you are wavering, or thinking of putting off your stop date, let me remind you of certain statistics about smoking and some immediate benefits of giving up. I hope these will convince you that NOW is the right time to carry through with your intentions.

If you continue to smoke cigarettes, here are the risks:

- You will be twelve times more likely to die from lung cancer.
- You will be ten times more likely to die from other lung diseases.
- You will be ten times more likely to die from cancer of the larynx.
- You will be six times more likely to die from cancer of the mouth.
- You will be twice as likely to die of heart disease.
- You will be twice as likely to die of a stroke.

Reflect for a moment: wouldn't it be extremely important for you to increase your chances, from two to twelve times, of gaining many extra healthy, happy, pain-free years in place of the long-term suffering and financial hardship associated with this list of illnesses?

But you don't have to wait many years to be aware of the good you do yourself by stopping. There are some immediate benefits that you can find out for yourself by just asking any successful quitter how he or she feels. They will most likely tell you, as one recently told me, 'It's an ego builder. You feel like a different person.'

Now let's talk about self-confidence. How can you increase confidence in your ability to be successful?

First of all, you need to be able to answer this question:

What will you do to resist the desire to smoke each time it hits you, and will you be able to do it until the urge passes?

When the craving for a cigarette descends on you, you need some 'short-range artillery' to shoot it down.

I have the perfect weapons for you, and I'll show you how to use them in the 7 + 7 Programme. With these weapons you *will* be able to resist the desire to smoke each time it hits you, and you *will* be able to do it until the urge passes.

Second, and more important in the long run, is that you need to be able to deal with your underlying reasons for smoking. What kind of satisfaction – physical, mental and emotional – has smoking been providing?

Here is a brief quiz to determine why you are (or formerly were) smoking cigarettes.

QUIZ 2 · MY MOST IMPORTANT REASONS FOR SMOKING

Circle the appropriate number:

1 = Never
2 = Sometimes
3 = Frequently
4 = Always

1. a. I smoke when I need a pickup.	1	2	3	4
b. I smoke to stop me slowing down.	1	2	3	4

2. a. I smoke for the pleasure of it.	1	2	3	4
b. I like to light up when I am comfortable and relaxed.	1	2	3	4

3. a. I smoke when I'm angry.	1	2	3	4
b. I smoke when I'm anxious.	1	2	3	4
c. I smoke when I'm tense.	1	2	3	4
d. I smoke when I'm depressed	1	2	3	4

4. a. I get anxious when I think I might run out of cigarettes.	1	2	3	4
b. I get anxious if I must go somewhere I will not be able to smoke when I really want to.	1	2	3	4

5. a. I smoke a cigarette within thirty minutes after I get up in the morning.	1	2	3	4
b. I smoke when I'm not feeling well.	1	2	3	4
c. I smoke a pack (or more) a day.	1	2	3	4

6. a. Sometimes I smoke just to keep my hands busy.	1	2	3	4
b. I smoke when I am bored.	1	2	3	4

Each of the questions in Quiz 2 reflects a different emphasis in your need for cigarettes. Usually, smokers rate questions in two or more of the different groups at the 3 or 4 level. If this applies to you, you will have to learn to cope with a number of different feelings and situations without the help of cigarettes.

A high rating on one or both of the questions in Group 1 suggests that you use cigarettes for stimulation or extra energy. For example, you may smoke to stay alert or for a boost while doing things that require concentration or extra effort of any kind. Cigarettes may help you stay awake when your body says it's time to sleep, but you have work to finish.

A high rating on one or both questions in Group 2 suggests that smoking adds to the pleasure of relaxing – physically, mentally or both. You may use cigarettes during work breaks, after finishing a tough job, or when you settle back for a cup of coffee or alcoholic beverage.

A high rating on one or more questions in Group 3 suggests that smoking is used to help you deal with negative effect. Smoking makes you feel better when something causes you to be angry, tense, anxious or depressed.

The questions in Group 4 reflect psychological dependency. You worry about running out of cigarettes before it happens and before you suffer any form of nicotine deprivation.

A high rating on questions in Group 5 suggests a chemical addiction. If you answered all three with a high rating, it means that without a periodic 'hit' you soon begin to experience withdrawal symptoms and feel quite uncomfortable.

A high rating on the questions in Group 6 suggests that smoking is something to do with your hands when you are nervous or uncomfortable, perhaps in social situations, maybe in place of eating. Or you may light up simply as something to do when you are bored, when having nothing to do makes you fidgety.

The different categories of questions in the above quiz show the great variety of gratifications that smoking can provide to different people with different needs. Nicotine is a versatile and powerful drug! It is more addicting than heroin or cocaine. And cigarette manufacturers have recently been accused of manipulating the nicotine content of their cigarettes, adding nicotine if necessary to maintain a constant predetermined amount in each cigarette, so that once you choose your brand you will get the same dose of the drug each time you smoke![1] Is it any wonder that so many millions have become dependent on nicotine, and that it is so difficult to stop smoking?

I will give you a brief but thorough description of the mechanisms through which nicotine exerts its powerful effects in the next chapter. But right now, in advance, I want to assure you that whatever *your* main reasons for smoking, the 7 + 7 Programme will give you a whole new set of strategies for obtaining satisfaction equal to or greater than the satisfaction you now obtain from nicotine, without any of the life-threatening dangers of smoking cigarettes.

[1]According to *Business Week*, 14 March 1994, a memo circulated internally at one of the major cigarette manufacturers contains the following: 'Without nicotine . . . there would be no smoking . . . Think of the cigarette as a dispenser for a unit dose of nicotine.'

2

Know Your Enemy

What is it that makes cigarette smoking so addictive?

If you smoke more than a few cigarettes a day, why do you feel so lousy when you try to stop?

Why does your appetite increase when you stop smoking?

And how, for goodness' sake, even if you don't eat a single crumb more than before you stop smoking, is it *still* possible for you to gain weight?

Nicotine elicits some powerful biochemical reactions that have an almost instantaneous effect on your mood, your cognitive abilities, your appetite and your metabolism. Since nicotine can result in pleasant feelings and its impact can actually be helpful in certain situations, it is easy to become physically and psychologically dependent on cigarettes.

Some smoking cessation experts like to differentiate the degree of dependence on cigarettes into several levels, depending on how much and when you smoke. Of course, the more you smoke, the more your body adjusts its chemistry to high levels of nicotine intake, which can lead to a true chemical dependence. However, even light smokers can become just as dependent on cigarettes because of nicotine's psychological impact, that is, the way it affects their mood and their feelings in certain situations. This can lead to a strong psychological dependency specific to those situations, and can be independent of the actual amount smoked each day. It turns out that the severity of withdrawal symptoms when you stop can be just as severe as a result of psychological dependency among light to moderate smokers as it can be as a result of chemical dependency among heavy smokers. Finally, because of the complexity of factors involved, moderate smokers are likely to gain as much weight as, or even more than, heavy smokers when they stop.

I'm going to start by explaining how nicotine brings about the physiological and psychological reactions that contribute to your underlying reasons for smoking. You will then understand the physiological basis for the answers you gave to the quizzes in the previous chapter, and you will understand why you need to follow the 7 + 7 Programme to compensate for these reactions when you give up smoking.

THE BIOCHEMICAL EFFECTS OF NICOTINE

It's only a matter of seconds before the impact of nicotine from the first puffs of a cigarette is felt in the central nervous system and throughout your body. There are nicotine receptors in several parts of the brain, one of which increases arousal when stimulated by nicotine and can help you think more clearly. Other receptors lie in a 'pleasure' centre of the brain which, when stimulated by nicotine, can make you feel more relaxed and less anxious.

The impact of nicotine is very powerful because it affects many different neurotransmitters and hormones that were designed to help a person cope with dangers of all kinds. Levels of catecholamines (epinephrine, norepinephrine and dopamine), beta-endorphin and cortisol in the central nervous system and bloodstream increase with each puff of a cigarette. These substances are mobilized whenever a person is injured or stressed in any way, physically or mentally. Thus, when you smoke a cigarette, the biochemicals that are secreted can help you feel less tense and more able to cope with whatever is stressing you. It takes just one cigarette (or for some people, two) for these neurohormonal substances in your body to reach an effective level.

The impact of these hormones lasts a certain amount of time after you've finished your cigarette because they keep circulating in your bloodstream. However, after each cigarette, your body goes to work to eliminate the excess and return to its normal baseline levels. You can become addicted to or dependent on the physical and psychological effects of these naturally occurring chemicals in the body which are stimulated by nicotine just as you can to amphetamines, heroin and other painkillers, which are chemically similar to epinephrine, norepinephrine, beta-endorphin and cortisol.

There tends to be a difference in the physiological, or chemical, dependency on nicotine between light and heavy smokers. Light smokers tend to use cigarettes only when they feel the need for nicotine's psychological impact, for example, to help deal with stress while working on a particular problem or to relax after dealing with it. They may use a cigarette to help reduce the initial tension in social situations, such as when they arrive at a cocktail party, or because a cigarette enhances the pleasure associated with a cup of coffee or an alcoholic drink. After a time, smoking can become a habit in these situations even when the psychological need is absent – you just automatically reach for a cigarette when you find yourself in a particular place doing a particular thing at a particular time.

Heavy smokers have become chemically dependent on heightened levels of hormones, stimulated by nicotine, which can have 'addicting' qualities. They need a cigarette with a certain periodicity, starting within thirty minutes or so after they get up in the morning. Then, as the level of hormones stimulated by each cigarette falls, they need another 'hit'. It can be every twenty, thirty or forty minutes, but if more than that period of time goes by, they begin to crave a cigarette.

Both light smokers, when denied the psychological support of nicotine in accustomed situations, and heavy smokers, when denied their periodic nicotine hit for even twenty-four hours, can begin to experience one or more characteristics of the withdrawal syndrome: anxiety, restlessness, irritability, cigarette cravings, inability to concentrate, dysphoria, hunger and drowsiness followed by insomnia when they try to fall asleep at night. Is it any wonder it's hard to stop!

But why does cigarette smoking help to control your weight, and why do most people gain weight when they stop? Is it simply a lack of willpower or self-control?

WHY SMOKING CESSATION IS LIKELY TO LEAD TO WEIGHT GAIN

Unfortunately, cigarette smoking really is an aid to weight management. Here is how it works and why it is so effective.

Nicotine can reduce your desire to eat by directly affecting the activity of serotonin and dopamine, which are substances that control neural transmission in areas of your brain that turn your appetite on and off. Nicotine elevates the activity of these substances in a way that is somewhat similar to what happens when you eat a sweet; for a certain period after smoking a cigarette or eating that sweet you feel less hungry.

Nicotine causes your adrenal glands to release catecholamines which in turn cause the liver to release glucose into the bloodstream and your fat cells to release fatty acids. This increases the energy available to all the cells of your body, and the reaction is similar to what happens after you eat, which also may help reduce your appetite.

The catecholamines are stimulants and they cause your metabolic rate to increase sharply within seconds after you begin smoking. The increase appears to be even greater during physical activity than when you are sitting still. If you smoke a pack or a pack and a half of cigarettes each day, your daily energy needs can be increased by about 200 calories. Some experts believe that a good part of this increase is due to the higher rate at which those fatty acids keep circulating in and out of your fat cells each time you smoke. That is, out come the fatty acids at the onset of smoking, and then back they go into the fat cells in between cigarettes. This work requires energy.

But there are a couple of even more insidious factors at work that can lead to weight gain when you stop smoking even though you don't eat an ounce more of anything. In fact, these factors can lead to weight gain even if you go on a reduced-calorie diet after you stop.

First, nicotine can cause an increase in the activity of the enzyme adipose tissue lipoprotein lipase (AT-LPL), which is responsible for incorporating fat into your fat cells. This appears to be a counter-regulatory reaction and it's likely that the more you smoke, the greater the increase in this fat-storing enzyme. I want to explain this in more detail because, if you are one of those people who is likely to gain weight, I think it will add to your motivation to do what it takes to stop smoking without suffering that consequence.

Because nicotine increases metabolic rate and keeps pulling fatty acids from your fat cells and burning them up each time you smoke a cigarette, smoking can result in your being from 10 to 12 pounds (4½ to 5½k), or even more, *below* the natural weight that you would have as a non-smoker. Your body tries to compensate for this nicotine-induced fat burning by working extra hard, increasing AT-LPL activity, to get what fat it can from your diet into your fat cells. The increased cycling of fatty acids in and out of your fat cells in between cigarettes may also stimulate heightened AT-LPL activity. The extent of AT-LPL activity may be related to the amount smoked: the more you smoke, the greater the cycling, and the greater the AT-LPL activity.

When you stop smoking, the heightened activity of AT-LPL[1] can make fat incorporation much easier than if you had never been a smoker. Your hungry fat cells are just lying in wait to suck up the fat in your diet, in order to make up for the depletion that they have endured due to nicotine.

Second, besides the increased likelihood of gaining weight from the fat in your diet when you stop smoking, *recent research suggests that there may also be an increased likelihood of gaining weight from the carbohydrates you eat*, which does not occur in non-smokers. Because this research is so new, and because it may be especially important for heavy smokers who have a hereditary tendency to obesity, I want to go into some detail on this particular possibility.

Here is some background.

In order to be used or stored as energy, the carbohydrates that you eat are converted to glucose. The body stores only a small amount of glucose, about half in your muscle cells and the rest in your liver. In this way, whenever you need energy for moving around, some glucose is immediately available in the muscles themselves, and the glucose stored in the liver can be secreted into the bloodstream almost instantaneously to back up the muscles' supply. In any given day, when you are at a stable weight, *almost none of the carbohydrate calories you eat is ever turned to fat for storage.* Daily fluctuations in carbohydrate intake are almost completely handled in the body by increasing and decreasing stores of glucose, not fat. *In order to gain fat weight from*

---

[1] How long this effect may last is not predictable in any given case. It may last weeks or months, and it may be responsible for just a few pounds of extra fat in one person and a great many pounds in another.

excess carbohydrate, you must continually outeat your energy needs by a considerable amount, day after day. This is true for both smokers and non-smokers.[1]

But here is the difference for smokers.

The hormone that controls the rate at which glucose is transported into the cells of your body is *insulin*. The more insulin circulating in your bloodstream, the faster glucose gets removed from your bloodstream and transported into your body cells. *The recent research I am talking about shows that smoking can depress insulin activity.* Thus, compared with non-smokers, the circulating levels of glucose in smokers will tend to be higher. Since the daily energy need of smokers is also higher, a good portion if not all of the extra glucose will be burned off and is not available either for storage in the muscles and liver or for conversion to fat.

When you stop smoking, *your circulating insulin level may go up*, which will make it easier for glucose to be transported into your muscles and liver. The immediate result is that your muscles and liver will simply store more than their normal, pre-cessation levels of glucose. Because of the high volume of water that combines with glucose when it goes into storage, you can gain 3 to 5 pounds in a day or two.

At that point, however, your liver and muscles are stuffed to capacity. Where is excess glucose going to go

[1] Most people store between 2000 and 4000 calories in glucose, compared with 50,000 to 200,000, or even more, calories in fat. Glucose is stored in a ratio of 1 part glucose to 4 parts water, while fat is stored in a ratio of about 4 parts fat to 1 part water. It takes about 400 calories of glucose combined with water to add a pound of weight to your body, while it takes 3500 calories in fat plus water to add a pound of weight. But the maximum storage of glucose can only add between 3 and 5 pounds (2 to 3k) to anybody's weight. Then, if excess intake continues and is not burned off, it can become available for conversion to fat.

if it can't get into your muscles and liver?

Excess glucose then becomes available for conversion to fat. And, in this connection, it becomes very important to remember that you may experience a decrease in total energy needs of up to 200 calories a day or even more when you stop smoking due to a decrease in your metabolic rate. So, if you continue your previous carbohydrate intake after you stop smoking, you will have an excess amount of glucose circulating in your bloodstream that has nowhere to go, except to be converted to fat and end up in your fat cells!

In other words, if, when you stop smoking, you eat just as you did before as a smoker, and don't find a way to burn up those surplus calories, including carbohydrate calories, you can first experience a quick gain in water weight and then *a portion of what was your customary carbohydrate intake can now end up as fat!*

So, talk about points piled up against you! As a result of biochemical changes, when you stop smoking:

1. Your body's tendency to store dietary fat may go up.
2. Your body's tendency to store carbohydrates, either as glucose or as fat, may also go up.
3. Your total energy needs can go down about 200 calories a day.
4. And, if three blows aren't enough, your appetite may increase, especially your taste for sweets! Here are the reasons for this phenomenon.

SMOKING CESSATION AND APPETITE

There are at least three reasons why quitters report an increase in appetite after stopping, with a particular increase in their desire for sweet foods.

First, one of the reasons you continue to smoke may be as a means of weight control, and you may reach for a cigarette just to have something other than food in your hands and mouth. It's a habit that may have developed to replace snacking when you take a break from work or when you first notice that you are just a little hungry in between meals, but not yet ready for lunch or dinner.

Second, if you tend to eat when you are nervous, and find that eating has a quieting, calming effect (which is a normal reaction, noted in most animals), you may have become accustomed to cigarettes for the same tension-reducing impact you would otherwise get from food. When you stop smoking, the desire to eat can now become overwhelming whenever you become tense.

Third, nicotine and carbohydrate foods, especially sweet foods, have a similar effect on serotonin activity in the brain. So, when you stop smoking, the substitution of a sweet can replace the biochemical impact of nicotine. This is a two-edged reaction: the eating of something sweet can help reduce the craving for a cigarette, *and it can help you be successful as a quitter*. The trick would be in finding a way to satisfy any sweet craving that occurs without adding to the difficulties you face in preventing weight gain.

Although studies show that appetite increases after giving up smoking, *the increase in caloric intake that occurs does not account for all the weight that is gained*. In quitters who gain weight, only about 70 per cent of the gain is, on average, due to increased food intake. People gain about 30 per cent more weight than can be directly attributed to the added calories they have eaten. This unfortunate 30 per cent 'bonus' weight gain is due to the metabolic changes that occur after you stop smoking, of which the three most likely are the decrease in metabolic rate, the residual increase in AT-LPL activity, and the increase in the rate of glucose storage.

SO, WHAT TO DO?

I have gone into such detail about the impact of nicotine, especially on your weight, for several reasons. To begin with, you deserve a full explanation that does not downplay the problems associated with quitting. It's not as easy as it's made out to be, especially coping with your body's tendency to gain weight. There is no need to feel inferior or guilty because you somehow lack 'will-power'. When you consider the power of the drug:

IT'S NOT YOUR FAULT THAT YOU FEEL HUNGRY WHEN YOU STOP.

IT'S NOT YOUR FAULT YOUR METABOLIC RATE DECREASES.

IT'S NOT YOUR FAULT THAT YOUR BODY RESPONDS TO NICOTINE WITHDRAWAL WITH AN INCREASE IN INSULIN, AND YOU'VE ALSO GOT THAT RESIDUAL INCREASED AT-LPL ACTIVITY CAUSED BY SMOKING.

These are biological, not moral, issues! They are the usual, NORMAL reactions to nicotine use and to stopping smoking.

However, my most important reason for going into such detail is that I believe you need to understand the rationale for each and every step that you must take to counter all of these physical and psychological effects. *How to Stop Smoking Without Gaining Weight* will show you exactly what you need to do and what you are accomplishing when you do it. And this will increase and maintain your motivation to keep doing it.

We are now ready for the 7 + 7 Programme for smokers who want to stop without gaining weight. *If you have already stopped smoking, you must still read these two chapters*. They contain advice that will help you continue to be a successful non-smoker, as well as many nutritional suggestions that are as helpful for losing weight as they are for preventing weight gain when you stop. Study these next two chapters first, and then begin the Ex-Smoker's Weight-Management Programme in Chapter 5.

The diet and activity programme present in *How to Stop Smoking Without Gaining Weight* is safe for people in good health. However, before changing your diet and starting an exercise programme you should check with your doctor to make sure the changes are suitable in your particular case. In addition, because nicotine interacts with a number of prescription and non-prescription drugs, magnifying or diminishing their impact, if you take any medication regularly it is essential to check with your doctor before you stop smoking so that dosages of these interacting medications can be adjusted if necessary.

3

How to Stop Smoking Without Gaining Weight: The 7 + 7 Programme

PART 1: MANAGING YOUR WEIGHT

You can make sure you won't gain weight when you stop smoking by completing Part 1 of the 7 + 7 Programme *before you stop*. (If you have already stopped, you should still read this chapter and Chapter 4 before going on to the Ex-Smoker's Weight-Management Programme since they contain important information for you as well as for smokers about to stop.)

Programmes that suggest you stop smoking and *then* go on a diet to lose weight are self-defeating. Seeing yourself gaining weight while you are struggling to remain a non-smoker is stressful enough, but going on a diet to lose weight after you have stopped smoking simply adds more stress to the stress already involved in smoking cessation. It's a fact: people who gain weight when they stop smoking and then try to adhere to a strict weight-loss diet *while they are still struggling to resist cigarettes* are more likely to relapse and start smoking again.

This will not happen to you when you use the 7 + 7 Programme.

The 7 + 7 Programme is a two-part programme designed to be as stress-free as possible as you undertake the difficult job of stopping smoking. Each part normally takes seven days, but you can take longer if you feel the need for more practice, or you can jump ahead whenever you feel ready. You're the boss. My aim is to show you how to be in complete control and 'stay cool' in situations where people who try to stop smoking feel frustrated and panic.

In Part 1 I will show you everything you need to do to prevent weight gain when you stop smoking. In Part 2 I will focus on smoking itself, and lead you through what research has shown to be the most effective approach to smoking cessation. If you have any doubts about your ability to kick the smoking habit, learning what you need to do to manage your weight *before* you stop will demonstrate that, given the right approach, you have the ability to change your behaviour in some very significant ways. This demonstration will give you all the confidence you need to deal with cigarettes.

Your task in Part 1 of the programme is to have all of your weapons *firmly in place* to combat a decrease in metabolic rate, an increase in the likelihood of fat and possibly carbohydrate storage, and a potential increase in your appetite, especially for sweet foods, one or all of which can occur when you stop smoking.

In the next seven days you will do this by:

1. Decreasing the fat in your diet while choosing the most healthy carbohydrate foods.
2. Starting an exercise programme that will burn off any excess fat and carbohydrate in your diet that might otherwise be forced into storage by the heightened activity of AT-LPL that has occurred as a result of having smoked cigarettes and the increase in insulin that occurs on stopping.

In addition, if you are a heavy smoker (a pack or more a day), I suggest you consult your doctor at some time during this first week about nicotine replacement therapy, so that you will be ready to use either the patch or the gum when you stop smoking in Part 2. Nicotine replacement therapy can help to minimize the metabolic changes that occur when you stop, as well as reduce withdrawal symptoms. Your doctor or pharmacist will tell you how to use the patch and I will summarize instructions for nicotine gum in Part 2 to avoid any confusion about its use. Nicotine lozenges and tablets are also available.

HOW TO CUT THE FAT IN YOUR DIET

Cutting the fat in your diet is THE most important nutritional change you can make, and it is quite easy when you use a one-meal-at-a-time approach. You simply take a look at what you have been eating at each meal and as snacks, and substitute a few lower-fat alternatives. These substitutions serve a dual purpose.

First, they prevent your consuming any excess fat that your body can end up storing in your fat cells. Second, by reducing the amount of fat that's present in your meals, they force your body to depend more upon the carbohydrate in your diet for energy throughout the day. This can prevent any increase in glucose storage that may occur as a result of heightened insulin activity in previously heavy smokers. In fact, if you follow all the recommendations in the 7 + 7 Programme, you will most likely be able to *increase* the amount of foods low in fat and higher in carbohydrates. This is desirable because a high-carbohydrate diet can help you fight the urge to smoke. If you choose the right foods, you will, in spite of eating more carbohydrates, still consume *fewer* total calories than before, since you will probably not be able to eat enough to equal your previous high-fat caloric intake.

Take a look at Tables 1 to 4. They contain tips and suggestions for satisfying low-fat alternatives to high-fat foods for breakfast, lunch, dinner and snacks. Then study my suggestions for low-fat meals on pages 61 to 65.

TABLE 1 · BREAKFAST SUGGESTIONS

ALTERNATIVES

Instead of croissants or sweet rolls (12-20 g fat per serving), *substitute* whole-grain bread, pitta or fruit bread, rice cakes, bagels and home-made bran or fruit muffins (1–3 g fat per serving).

Instead of whole milk (8 g fat per cup/8 fl oz/225 ml), *substitute* skimmed or semi-skimmed milk (0–2 g per cup).

Instead of butter or margarine (4 g fat per scant teaspoon), *substitute* honey, jam or marmalade (0 fat), reduced-fat spreads (2–3 g fat per scant teaspoon) or cottage cheese (½–1 g per tablespoon).

Instead of fried or scrambled eggs (9 g fat each), boil or poach. Frying or scrambling adds 4 g fat per scant teaspoon of fat.

Instead of bacon (13 g fat per ¾ ounce/21 g, or 3 rashers grilled crisp, cooked weight), *substitute* the new reduced-fat turkey versions (1.1 g fat per ¾ ounce, cooked weight).

TIPS
Use a variety of ready-to-eat cereals (1–3 g fat per serving). Mix a high-fibre kind with a favourite lower-fibre one. Avoid highly sugared varieties and sweeten with fresh or dried fruit instead of sugar.

Flavour porridge or hot cereals with a touch of cinnamon or nutmeg, and add dried fruit.

Blend low-fat cottage cheese or yogurt cheese with salsa, onions, sardines, tinned salmon or various seasonings and use as a spread on rolls, toast or bagels. (Make yogurt cheese by allowing low-fat yogurt to drip through cheesecloth or a coffee filter suspended over a bowl overnight.)

Use Grapenuts or Rice Crispies to add crunchiness to yogurt, hot cereals or stewed fruit.

When eating out, ask for your roll, sandwich or toast to be served without butter or margarine. If you must, add a little at the table. Use syrup, jam or fruit instead of fat.

TABLE 2 · LUNCH SUGGESTIONS

ALTERNATIVES
Instead of croissants (12–20 g fat), *substitute* whole-grain

breads or rolls, bagels, pitta or French bread (1–2 g fat) for sandwiches.

Instead of high-fat luncheon meats such as spam or salami (6–8 g fat per ounce/28 g), *substitute* turkey, lean ham or chicken roll (1–2 g fat per ounce).

Instead of mayonnaise (11–12 g fat per dessertspoon) on sandwiches, *substitute* low-fat mayonnaise or salad dressing (2–5 g fat per dessertspoon) or, better, mustard or ketchup (0 fat).

Instead of high-fat dressings (6–9 g fat per dessertspoon) for salads, *substitute* no- or low-fat dressings (0–2 g fat per dessertspoon) or use only 1 teaspoon of a high-fat variety.

Instead of cream- or cheese-based soups (10–15 g fat per cup/ 8 fl oz/225 ml), *substitute* clear soups such as chicken noodle or consommé, or vegetable varieties (1–3 g fat per cup).

Instead of potato crisps or cheese nibbles (10 g fat per ounce/28 g), *substitute* pretzels or breadsticks (1 g fat per ounce).

In place of high-fat sweet biscuits (2–4 g fat per biscuit or approx. ½ ounce), *substitute* low-fat crackers such as Ryvita, melba toast, matzohs or rice cakes (0–2 g fat per ½ ounce/14g).

Instead of regular cheese (8–10 g fat per ounce/28 g), *substitute* low-fat varieties (3–5 g fat per ounce) or, better yet, skip it altogether.

Instead of high-fat cakes or pastries (6–20 g fat per suggested serving), *substitute* fruit or muesli bars, or dried fruit (0–2 g fat per suggested serving).

TIPS
Cut up raw vegetables and store in water in an airtight

container in the refrigerator. They will stay fresh and crisp for lunches, snacks or cooking.

Keep a supply of tinned tuna (in brine), salmon, sardines and crabmeat. Try them with different condiments and low-fat dressings or as sandwich spreads.

Mix low-fat cottage cheese with dry soup mix, chopped onion, salsa or any of your preferred herbs or seasonings for sandwich spreads and salads.

When visiting a salad bar, fill up on vegetables, chick peas, beans and fruit. Take only small amounts of meats, cheese, eggs and mayonnaise-based salads.

TABLE 3 · DINNER SUGGESTIONS

THREE WAYS TO LOWER THE FAT CONTENT OF YOUR FAVOURITE RECIPES:

1. Substitute lower-fat ingredients.
2. Alter the basic method of preparation.
3. Reduce the amount of fat added.

FOR EXAMPLE:
1. Lean cuts of meat such as topside or silverside, *well-trimmed* sirloin, fillet or skirt. These and pork tenderloin have only a quarter to one-third the fat of shoulder meat or chops. If you don't trim well *before* cooking, the melted fat seeps between the lean muscle fibres and doubles the fat content of the cooked lean meat.

To tenderize lean meats, marinate for several hours with wine, soy sauce or fruit juice (anything slightly acidic) and seasonings.

Choose extra-lean beef mince or minced turkey (1–3 g fat per ounce) rather than ordinary mince (up to 10 g fat per ounce).

2. Use lower-fat preparation methods such as baking, roasting, grilling, poaching, steaming or boiling rather than frying or cooking in fat. Frying can increase the fat content from two to six times, depending on the use of flour or batter.

3. Unless you are working from a specifically designed low-fat recipe, use only one-third to half of the fat called for.

TIPS TO HELP YOU PUT THESE SUGGESTIONS INTO PRACTICE:

Flavour vegetables with herbs and seasonings rather than added fat. If you generally add meat fat to beans or vegetables, use an ounce or two of lean ham for a meaty flavour.

Stock these low-fat kitchen essentials: tinned consommé, vegetable bouillon, low-fat yogurt, tinned evaporated partly skimmed milk and an assortment of seasonings and spices.

Sauté vegetables in a nonstick pan with bouillon or wine rather than oil or butter. Warm a pan before greasing very lightly with a little oil on paper.

When using grated cheese (8–10 g fat per ounce/28 g) in a recipe, use less of a stronger cheese such as mature cheddar, or use a reduced-fat variety (4–5 g fat per ounce).

Blend low-fat cottage cheese with a touch of lemon juice for a creamy baked potato topping, or try low-fat yogurt spiked with herbs or finely diced red pepper. Use partly skimmed evaporated milk or skimmed milk with non-fat dry milk added for recipes that call for cream or whole milk.

Plan a meatless meal one or two nights a week. Try legumes and rice or pasta with a vegetable sauce.

Oven-fry instead of frying in fat – smear a warmed baking dish with vegetable fat and bake at a high temperature, turning at least once. Dip fish or chicken in low-fat milk or egg whites and coat with seasoned breadcrumbs.

When a recipe calls for tinned cream soup, replace at least half the quantity with partly skimmed evaporated milk plus corn-flour or flour added as a thickener.

Basic everyday, low-fat desserts include fresh or stewed fruit, low-fat yogurt and yogurt drinks, sorbet and dried fruits.

TABLE 4 · SNACK SUGGESTIONS

ALTERNATIVES

Instead of chocolate (13–14 g fat per serving), *substitute* jelly beans, gumdrops, lemon drops, polo mints or liquorice (0 fat).

Instead of potato crisps and cheese snacks (10–14 g fat per serving), *substitute* pretzels, rice cakes or bagels (0–1 g fat per serving).

Instead of regular and dairy ice cream (8–20 g fat per serving), *substitute* sorbets and low-fat frozen yogurt (0–3 g fat per serving).

Instead of nuts, including peanuts (10–14 g fat per serving), *substitute* popcorn (2 g fat per serving).

Instead of chocolate-chip, cream-filled or other fatty biscuits (4–6 g fat each), *substitute* fruit bars, rice cakes or dried fruit (0–1g fat each).

Instead of croissants or butteries (10–20 g fat each), *substitute* whole-grain rolls, pitta bread or bagels (1–4 g fat each).

Instead of Danish pastries, doughnuts, pies and iced or cream cakes (10–20 g fat each serving), *substitute* fruit bread and bagels (1–3 g fat).

TIPS
Fresh and dried fruit are your best sweet snacks and should be your first choices for sweets.

Vegetables such as carrot and celery sticks, sweet peppers and courgettes are good, crunchy choices.

ESPECIALLY FOR SMOKERS
Instead of smoking a cigarette, suck ONE hard sweet or chew gum. But if eating one boiled sweet or peppermint turns on your appetite for sweets, eat instead a piece of fruit or a serving of low-fat crackers, such as Ryvita or melba toast, as your in-between-meal snack.

Many people who stop smoking find that the instructions I've just given are all they need to put an effective programme into practice. If you hate keeping records of everything you eat and can make the changes I've just suggested without writing everything down, this informal approach may work for you. You are ready to begin! Just follow my recommendations in the food tables and, in addition, look up the fat content of the foods you normally eat as you go through the next seven days so that you can use specific low-fat alternatives for these foods. Use the Fat and Carbohydrate Counter in Appendix C. Instead of high-fat versions, choose low-fat dairy products, lean cuts of meat, low-fat desserts and snacks, and plenty of fruit, vegetables and grain products. If, at the end of seven days, you have made satisfying substitutes at all your meals and for snacks, and are following my suggestions for physical activity below, you will be ready to go on to

Part 2 in the next chapter. However:

Would you like a guarantee that your approach will work?

You can *guarantee* that you are making the changes in
your diet that will enable you to stop smoking without
gaining weight by becoming a little more scientific. But
before showing you how to do this, I need to review
some nutritional guidelines and explain why you need
to think in terms of grams of fat in your diet to imple-
ment these guidelines, rather than percentages.

If you are like most people in the Western world,
your present diet contains more fat than is good for you,
whether you smoke or not. Health authorities without
exception recommend that you obtain no more than 30
per cent of your calories from fat, while a majority recommend that you decrease to 20 or 25 per cent.[1]
Between 60 and 65 per cent of your calories should be
obtained from carbohydrate, and about 10 to 15 per cent
from protein. But very few people need to be concerned
about their intake of carbohydrate or protein when they
reduce their fat calories. When you cut the fat content
of your diet, and substitute the high-carbohydrate
foods that I recommend, carbohydrate and protein percentages take care of themselves without any special
attention or further calculations.

In practice, it is much simpler to set a target for fat
consumption each day in terms of total grams rather
than beat your brains out trying to average the
percentage of fat from a day's eating from foods that

---

[1] If you already suffer from cardiovascular disease, you might do
even better reducing your intake of fat to as low as 10 per cent.
However, this drastic a change in your diet should be discussed with
your doctor before you make it.

contain different percentages based on a different number of calories. For example, try calculating the percentage of fat in the following healthy dinner, averaged across the three dishes:

Baked sole with a scant teaspoon of butter and a squeeze of lemon: 202 calories, 37 per cent fat

Medium baked potato with a scant teaspoon of butter: 238 calories, 16 per cent fat

1 serving of steamed broccoli: 46 calories, 8 per cent fat

Quick: What's the percentage fat content of this meal?

Can you imagine trying to work this out for an entire day, day after day?

It is far easier to think in terms of grams of fat per day than it is to average percentages. For example, if you are a woman who can maintain her weight by eating around 1600 calories per day, a target of 25 per cent fat would be 44 grams. By looking up the fat content in the Fat and Carbohydrate Counter in Appendix C, you would quickly discover that the above meal contains 11 grams of fat. You would have 33 to go to meet your daily target of 44 grams. Apart from simply adding the grams of fat in each dish, no mathematical operation is required.[1]

Under normal circumstances, if you were not under the gun with respect to fat intake while you are giving up smoking, you would choose a target for daily fat intake from Table 5 (page 58), which contains the

---

[1] This illustrative meal contains 486 calories, of which 99 are obtained from fat (11 grams of fat x 9 calories per gram = 99 calories). Thus, about 20 per cent of the calories in the meal come from fat.

amount of fat in grams for different percentages of total calories. A woman who can maintain desirable weight on 1800 calories and who wishes to choose a healthy target of 25 per cent of calories from fat would set an upper limit of 50 grams per day; a man on a diet of 2200 calories would aim for 61 grams.

However, as a person about to stop smoking, you have a special problem. You must compensate for a possible metabolic slowdown that can equal as much as 200 calories per day (or more in heavy smokers), plus a possible tendency on the part of your fat cells to suck up fat from your diet to the tune of about another 100 calories a day. In other words, we must find a way to eliminate or burn up about 300 calories a day to prevent you from gaining weight.

Our two primary weapons are cutting the fat in the diet and increasing physical activity. I suggest you aim to consume at least 20 grams of fat less per day than you are doing now. That will equal about 180 fewer calories in fat available for storage. If cutting 20 grams of fat from your present diet leaves you consuming more than 25 per cent of calories from fat, cut more. It is even better to reduce fat consumption to 20 per cent of calories, but in no circumstances should a woman cut below 20 grams of fat a day or a man below 30 grams without a medical reason and the supervision of a qualified health professional. Your body needs a small amount of fat in your diet in order to carry out basic metabolic functions.

What about carbohydrates?

Excess carbohydrates are not likely to become a problem for most people who stop smoking when they follow the preceding instructions for reducing fat consumption. However, in order to be sure that you won't gain weight, you must monitor your intake of carbohydrate as well as fat, at least until you determine that your consumption is not going to cause you any difficulty.

As I explained previously, some smokers may experience a difficulty with carbohydrate consumption because of an increase in insulin activity as a result of giving up cigarettes. This in turn may result in a temporary increase in the amount of glucose that is stored in your muscles and liver. This is really water weight and, while it may temporarily amount to several pounds, it is not likely to end up as fat weight. Unless you outeat your total daily energy needs by a considerable amount, day after day, almost no carbohydrate in your diet is converted to fat for storage. So focus on decreasing your fat intake and making sure your carbohydrate intake does not continually exceed your daily energy needs, and you will see no permanent weight gain. Of course, you can add an additional guarantee that your carbohydrate intake will not exceed your energy needs by following my recommendations for physical activity, which, by the way, will also help prevent excess water retention.

The real problem with carbohydrates is likely to occur only for people who develop a craving for sweet things when they stop smoking. While many quitters find that a hard sweet, such as a polo mint, is an excellent way to fend off the immediate desire for a cigarette, some people lose control of themselves and begin to eat anything in which the calories come entirely from sugar. Instead of finding that one satisfies, once they start, they can't stop until they finish the whole bag.

In part this reaction may also be related to changes in insulin activity. It occurs because these people experience what's called an 'insulin overshoot'. Their bodies react to sugar by secreting more insulin than is actually required to maintain normal levels of glucose in their bloodstream. Soon after consuming anything in which all the calories come from sugar, such as the boiled sweets which might otherwise be useful, the excess insulin reduces their blood sugar below normal, they become temporarily hypoglycaemic, and they begin to crave more sugar just to return to normal. It becomes a vicious cycle.

If you already know from past experience that it's hard to contain your desire for sweets once you start to eat them, or if it begins to happen to you when you experiment with sucking a boiled sweet or mint in place of a cigarette, you must avoid straight sugar sweets or sugar-sweetened gum. Instead, you should maintain a normal blood sugar level by eating a healthy three meals a day and snacking three times a day on complex-carbohydrate foods. Because complex carbohydrates are more slowly converted to glucose, they are not so likely to cause an insulin overshoot and the cyclic reaction that leads to increased sugar consumption. My best recommendations for snacks are listed in Table 4 on page 51.

HOW TO SET A TARGET FOR FAT AND CARBOHYDRATE CONSUMPTION IN ORDER TO STOP SMOKING WITHOUT GAINING WEIGHT

Step 1. For the first two of the next seven days, keep a record of your fat and carbohydrate intake in grams, together with total calories, *without making any changes* in your diet. Use the Fat and Carbohydrate Counter in Appendix C and keep this record as part of the Seven-Day Eating Record at the end of this chapter.[1]

Step 2. Starting on Day 3, use Table 5 to set a fat goal in grams that is between 20 and 25 per cent of your average total calories, or at least 20 grams below your baseline of the previous two days, whichever is lower. *(Remember, do not go below 20 grams of fat per day if you are a woman or 30 grams if you are a man.)*

TABLE 5 · FAT-GRAM TOTALS FOR DIFFERENT PERCENTAGES OF TOTAL CALORIES

TOTAL CALORIES	Grams of total fat as a percentage of total calories:		
	20%	25%	30%
1200	27	33	40
1300	29	36	43
1400	31	39	47
1500	33	42	50
1600	36	44	53
1700	38	47	57
1800	40	50	60
1900	42	53	63
2000	44	56	67
2100	47	58	70
2200	49	61	73
2300	51	64	77
2400	53	67	80
2500	56	69	83
2600	58	72	87
2700	60	75	90

[1]You can photocopy this Seven-Day Eating Record to use the next week and as long as you like. You will also find another, Fourteen-Day Eating Record in Chapter 5 which will carry you through the next two weeks, after you have stopped smoking.

Set your daily target for carbohydrates, tentatively, at the average of your two-day baseline level, with the following flexibility in mind: if you cut 20 grams or more of fat from your diet, you may be able to add some carbohydrates. You will know in a couple of days whether you can do this, since by cutting the fat while you are still smoking, you may begin to lose weight.

If you find that you can add some carbohydrates to your diet at this time, begin to do it as snacks. When you stop smoking, snacking on carbohydrate foods throughout the day can help to allay the craving for cigarettes.

By following my recommendations for physical activity, which can make sure that you do not outeat your daily energy needs, you may find, as most people do, that you can actually add as many carbohydrate grams back to your diet as you have cut in fat, or even more, since carbohydrates contain only 4 calories per gram, whereas fat contains 9 calories per gram. Replacing fat with carbohydrates in your diet, in the form of fruit, vegetables and grains, is basically desirable if you have been eating the typical Western high-fat diet, since it will help you reach nutritional guidelines of 60 to 65 per cent of total calories from carbohydrates. You can refer to Table 6 on the following page to determine the amount of carbohydrates in grams for different percentages of total calories.

TABLE 6 · CARBOHYDRATE-GRAM TOTALS FOR DIFFERENT PERCENTAGES OF TOTAL CALORIES

TOTAL CALORIES	Grams of total carbohydrate as a percentage of total calories		
	55%	60%	65%
1200	165	180	195
1300	179	195	211
1400	193	210	228
1500	206	225	244
1600	220	240	260
1700	234	255	276
1800	248	270	293
1900	261	285	309
2000	275	300	358
2100	289	315	341
2200	303	330	358
2300	316	345	374
2400	330	360	390
2500	344	375	406
2600	359	390	423
2700	371	405	439

Now, what about those total calories?

Recall that you may need to compensate for a total of 300 calories in metabolic slowdown and increased fat incorporation when you stop smoking. By adding 300 calories of physical activity to your daily regimen you may be able to come out even – no decrease in total caloric intake and still no weight gain. However, I suggest you start with a balanced fifty-fifty combination: compensate in part on the energy-intake side by reducing total fat without a complete matching increase in carbohydrates, and on the energy-output side, increase physical activity. When you reach the final goal in physical activity, as discussed later in this chapter, you may indeed find you can increase calories back to your baseline level.

Step 3. Starting on Day 3 and for the next five days, before you begin Part 2 of the programme, begin to substitute low-fat foods at each meal and at snack times, according to the suggestions in Tables 1 to 4. Keep a record of your fat and carbohydrate intake, making sure you do not exceed your daily targets.

Here are some sample meals for breakfast, lunch and dinner. (My snack suggestions appear in Table 4 on page 51.) Suggestions highlighted in bold type refer to recipes in Chapter 6. The recipes contain additional nutritional information.

BASIC BREAKFASTS[1]

Breakfast 1

Orange, grapefruit, or tomato juice (0 fat)
Ready Brek with sliced fruit (1–3 g fat)
Skimmed or semi-skimmed milk (0–2 g fat per 4 fl oz/110 ml)
Slice of whole-grain toast (1 g fat; marmalade optional, 0 fat)
Beverage (1 g fat for 2 tablespoons whole milk)

Breakfast 2

Melon or other fresh fruit (0 fat)
Bagel, crusty brown roll or 2 slices toast (1–2 g fat)

[1] I have included estimates only for fat content in these suggested meals since that is the most important nutrient over which you must exercise control. The carbohydrate content can vary to a certain degree in each of these meals, depending on your selection when I give several options and on the quantity, so you must look up the carbohydrate content for the foods you eat to be accurate.

Jam or marmalade optional (0 fat)
Skimmed or semi-skimmed milk (0–2 g fat per cup)[1] OR
Beverage of your choice (1 g fat for 2 tablespoons whole milk)

Breakfast 3

Fruit or juice (0 fat)
Honey Bran Muffin (1 g fat) or 2 slices of fruit bread (2 g fat)
Jam or honey optional (0 fat)
Beverage (1 g fat for 2 tablespoons whole milk)

Breakfast 4

Fruit or juice (0 fat)
Porridge with cinnamon and raisins (2–4 g fat)
Toast (1 g fat per slice; jam optional, 0 fat)
Beverage (1 g fat for 2 tablespoons whole milk)

Special Breakfast 5

Choice of fruit (0 fat)
2 slices turkey bacon fried as recommended (2 g fat)
2 slices whole-grain toast
Jam, jelly or syrup (0 fat)
Beverage (1 g fat for 2 tablespoons whole milk)

BASIC LUNCHES

Lunch 1

Clear soup (1 g fat per cup)

---

[1] The cup measure used contains 8f.oz or 225ml.

Sandwich with 1 ounce/28 g sliced turkey or lean ham
(3 g fat; 0 fat for mustard or ketchup;
2 g fat for 1 dessertspoon low-fat mayonnaise)
Fruit or raw vegetables (0 fat)
Beverage (1 g fat for 2 tablespoons whole milk)

Lunch 2

Tuna or chicken salad
(3½ ounces/100 g, made with 1 dessertspoon low-fat
mayonnaise, 4 g fat)
Lettuce, assorted greens, fresh vegetables (0 fat)
Whole-wheat crispbreads (2–4 g fat)
Choice of fruit (0 fat)
Beverage (1 g fat for 2 tablespoons whole milk)

Lunch 3

Very low-fat yogurt with berries, banana or other
favourite fruit, mixed in blender (0–2 g fat)
Assorted raw vegetables (0 fat)
Whole-wheat crackers or pretzel sticks (2–4 g fat)
Beverage (1 g fat for 2 tablespoons whole milk)

Lunch 4

Baked potato served with 4 ounces/110 g low-fat
cottage cheese (2–4 g fat)
Diced spring onions and ketchup (optional, 0 fat)
Tossed salad with low-fat dressing (2 g fat)
Fruit (0 g fat)
Beverage (1 g fat for 2 tablespoons whole milk)

Lunch 5

Sardine sandwich
(2 slices wholemeal or pumpernickel bread, 2 ounces/
56 g tinned sardines, drained, plenty of your favourite
mustard, slice of tomato or lettuce, a few bean sprouts,
9 g fat)
Beverage (1 g fat for 2 tablespoons whole milk)

BASIC DINNERS

Dinner 1

Pasta with **Real Italian Tomato Sauce** (4 g fat)
Tossed salad with low-cal dressing (3 g fat)
Slice of Italian or French bread (1 g fat)
Seasonal fruit (0 fat)
Chocolate-Chip Cookie (5 g fat)

Dinner 2

Baked Bass with Lemon-Wine Bouillon (7 g fat)
Baked courgettes (1–2 courgettes, 0 fat; with 1 scant tea-
spoon butter, 4 g fat)
Brussels sprouts or other green vegetable (0 fat)
Low-fat frozen yogurt or sorbet (1–3 g fat)

Dinner 3

Marinated Steak (10 g fat)
Baked potato (0 fat)
Green beans with water chestnuts (0 fat)
Tossed salad with low-fat dressing (2 g fat)
Slice of whole-grain bread (1 g fat)
Citrus fruit cup (0 fat)

Dinner 4

Chicken Cacciatore (with 3 ounces/80 g (dry weight) spaghetti, 5 g fat)
Broccoli or other green vegetable (prepared your favourite way, 4 g fat for 1 scant teaspoon butter)
Tossed salad with low-fat dressing (2 g fat)
Thick slice of French or Italian bread (2 g fat)
Stewed or fresh fruit (0 fat)

Dinner 5

Vegetarian Chilli Texas Style (1 g fat)
Brown or wild rice (2 ounces/56 g (dry weight), 1 g fat)
Asparagus or other green vegetable
(4 g fat for 1 scant teaspoon butter)
Slice of wholemeal or rye bread (1 g fat)
Frozen low-fat yogurt or sorbet (1–3 g fat)

THE 7 + 7 ACTIVITY PROGRAMME

Previously sedentary people who included physical activity as part of their programme to stop smoking will tell you without exception that becoming active played a key role in their success. There are many reasons for this.

- When people become physically active, they also become more self-confident and like themselves better. The feeling of increased competence is pervasive and affects every aspect of their lives, including their ability to stop smoking.
- When people become active they feel more energetic, and, specifically, they feel more capable of dealing

with tension in their lives, without reliance on cigarettes.

- When people get active the smell of cigarette smoke often becomes offensive. Several months after stopping, ex-smokers who exercise daily will tell you that their bodies react somewhat violently if they inhale a cigarette or even sit next to someone who is smoking one.

- Finally, physical activity provides *the ultimate guarantee* that you won't gain weight when you stop smoking because it burns off the calories that were formerly burned off by smoking.

YOUR PHYSICAL ACTIVITY GOAL

On average, a pack of cigarettes per day increases your daily energy needs to maintain your weight by about 200 calories.

Forty-five minutes of moving about instead of sitting still will also increase your daily energy needs by about 200 calories.

I think you get the picture.

So the real question is how to become motivated to get active *and stay that way*. It's one thing to begin an activity programme. It's quite another to begin to think of yourself as 'an active person'. About 90 per cent of the people who begin an activity programme with periodic visits to a fitness centre or any other 'three-times-per-week' approach, as though it were a doctor's prescription, give up exercising within a year. For people who think of themselves as physically active, physical activity is part of their self-concept, and essential to the good feelings they have about themselves. Perhaps this comparison will make my meaning clearer: it's one thing to say 'I play tennis three times a week,' for the worthy purpose of staying slim and healthier, but quite another to say, 'I am a tennis player.'

The easiest way to become an active person, and to begin to think of yourself as an active person as part of your self-concept, is to build some kind of physical activity into your daily life. Begin by setting aside ten minutes *every day* for physical activity, and gradually increase the time to forty-five minutes, or more if your schedule permits. For example, go out from your home or workplace for a walk. Do it every day at the same time, if you can. At the end of about two weeks your walk will begin to feel like an essential part of your life. You will feel uncomfortable if you miss it, just as you do if you fail to brush your teeth at the customary time!

The occasional approach to activity, such as three times a week at the health club or participation in an occasional aerobics dance class, is certainly good for you, but by itself this approach will not become habitual and it will not lead to the fundamental change in the way you think about yourself that I am talking about. It takes doing something active *every day*. Of course, you can mix your activities. Take up an active sport, such as tennis, and alternate it with swimming, bicycling or gentle jogging (if you are not overweight and your doctor does not object for medical reasons). Rotate these different activities from day to day, but you must be regular.

To experience the full psychological benefits of exercise it takes being active in one continuous period of about forty-five minutes in some fairly vigorous activity. However, if your schedule doesn't permit this, you can still end up burning all the calories you need to burn to compensate for those that previously went up in smoke by just getting up out of your chair for five minutes every hour and moving about as briskly as your environment permits. Pace the hallways, climb a few flights of stairs, lift some light weights. Take every opportunity to increase the time your body is in motion. Every little bit helps. For example, make all appointments in other people's offices rather than your own, park as far as possible from any destination to which you drive and walk the remaining distance, choose a restaurant for lunch that requires a five- or ten-minute walk in each direction. Remind yourself that every five minutes of movement will burn about 25 calories. Even though this approach may not lead to a fundamental change in your self-concept, you will probably feel so much more energetic when you move about this way that it will become a part of your daily routine.

Table 7 contains the caloric energy expenditures for many different forms of physical activity. Aim to add physical activity requiring between 200 and 300 calories a day in energy expenditure to the movement that is otherwise required of you in your daily responsibilities.

TABLE 7 · APPROXIMATE ENERGY COSTS IN EACH 15 MINUTES OF VARIOUS ACTIVITIES*

Activity	Calories per 15 minutes
Aerobic dancing	105
Badminton	99
Ballroom dancing, continuous	53
Basketball	141
Canoeing (recreational)	45
Cleaning house (steady movement)	63
Climbing hills (steady pace)	123
Cooking dinner	47
Cycling	
5.5 mph, level ground	66
9.4 mph, level ground	102

Activity	Calories per 15 minutes
Football	135
Gardening (raking)	56
Golf (walking – no cart)	87
Gymnastics	88
Horseback riding	
walking	42
trotting	113
Judo	199
Piano playing	41
Rowing (machine, fast pace)	105
Running	
11 min. 30 sec. per mile	138
10 min. per mile	174
9 min. per mile	197
8 min. per mile	213
7 min. per mile	234
6 min. per mile	260
Skiing	
cross-country, walking pace	146
downhill	101
Squash	216
Swimming	
freestyle, moderate pace	143
sidestroke	125
Table tennis	69
Tennis	111
Typing (electric typewriter)	27
Volleyball	51
Walking	
3 mph, level ground	66
4 mph, level ground	99
downstairs, steady pace	50
upstairs, slow steady pace	151

*Energy costs are calculated for people weighing 150 pounds (14 stone 10 lbs/68 k). For each 10 pounds (4½ k). more or less, add or subtract 7 per cent, respectively, from these figures.

If you choose walking as your main way to increase physical activity, one way to stay motivated is to buy a pedometer at your local sports shop and keep track of your total mileage each day. If you work in a sedentary occupation, you probably total about 2 miles a day. To maintain your weight, and help stay in excellent health, you need to average at least 5 miles a day. (On days when you substitute some other activity for walking, the caloric expenditure will be approximately the same, minute for minute, so long as these other activities involve your whole body, such as swimming or cycling, and they are done at about the same intensity as your walk.)

Whenever you feel the urge to smoke after you have stopped, get up and move around or lift some light weights instead. Brief physical activity not only reduces the urge to smoke, it can give you the lift you might otherwise have obtained from nicotine.

THE IMPORTANCE OF STRENGTH TRAINING

Recent research has shown that anaerobic activities, such as light strength training, in combination with an aerobic activity, such as walking, can play a significant role in a smoking-cessation programme and help prevent weight gain.[1] When you walk at a steady, moderate pace you burn relatively more fat

---

[1] By definition, aerobic activities are done in the presence of oxygen. That is, your intake of oxygen keeps up with the need for oxygen. For example, when you walk at a moderate pace, you don't get out of breath and keep on breathing hard when you stop to make up for the oxygen deficit that occurs when you exercise more intensely. Anaerobic activities, such as lifting weights, use oxygen and the store of glucose in your muscles faster than they can be replaced – you go into oxygen deficit, you must take a rest and replenish the glucose in your muscles from the supply in your liver before you can repeat the activity, and you keep breathing harder for a time after you finish exertion.

than glucose in your fuel mixture. When you engage in strength training you burn relatively more glucose than fat. Between the two forms of activity you help to normalize the circulating levels of both fat and glucose in your bloodstream. Furthermore, by replacing a few pounds of fat tissue with muscle tissue, which is the usual consequence of exercise of both kinds but maximized with strength training, you increase your metabolic rate by a couple of percentage points around the clock. That's because, compared with fat cells, muscle cells are much more active and burn more calories even when you are sitting still or sleeping.

I suggest you purchase a set of light weights – 3 pounds (1.8 kilos) each for a woman and either 5 pounds or 3 kilos (6.6 pounds) each for a man – and begin the light strength-training programme in Appendix A (or simply follow the suggestions that come with the weights). Aim for ten minutes a day. In addition, keep the weights handy so that whenever you feel the urge to smoke you can use them for a few moments instead of lighting up a cigarette. I strongly encourage you to try this since you may find, like many others, that lifting light weights for three to five minutes completely eliminates your desire to smoke and leaves you with a much more invigorated and satisfying feeling than you used to get from smoking a cigarette.

KEEP A DAILY RECORD

Be sure you are meeting a daily activity goal of a minimum of forty-five minutes of extra aerobic physical activity, plus ten minutes of strength training, by keeping a Daily Activity Record. Use the form at the end of the chapter or devise your own. Keep an activity record, as well as an eating record, for at least three weeks after you stop smoking.

SEVEN-DAY EATING RECORD

Column Headings: FAT = FAT; CARB = CARBOHYDRATE; CAL = CALORIES. List the food you eat at all meals and for snacks. Look up the fat and carbohydrate grams, and the calories, in the Fat and Carbohydrate Counter in Appendix C. Keep

	DAY 1			DAY 2			DAY 3		
DATE BEGUN	FAT	CARB	CAL	FAT	CARB	CAL	FAT	CARB	CAL
BREAKFAST									
SNACK									
LUNCH									
SNACK									
DINNER									
SNACK									
Total									

Now we are ready to go on to Part 2 of the 7 + 7 Programme and do away with cigarettes.

this record for the next seven days. You may photocopy it to use thereafter, or use the Fourteen-Day Eating Record in Chapter 5. Continue to monitor your food consumption after you stop smoking for at least three weeks.

DAY 4			DAY 5			DAY 6			DAY 7		
F A T	C A R B	C A L	F A T	C A R B	C A L	F A T	C A R B	C A L	F A T	C A R B	C A L

SEVEN-DAY ACTIVITY RECORD

List all of your extra daily aerobic and strength-training activities, with starting and ending times. Aim for at least forty-five minutes of aerobic activity, such as walking or its equivalent, and a minimum of ten minutes of light strength training. Make photocopies and keep this record for at least three weeks after you stop smoking.

DATE BEGUN:	ACTIVITY	START TIME	END TIME
DAY 1			
DAY 2			
DAY 3			
DAY 4			
DAY 5			
DAY 6			
DAY 7			

4

How to Stop Smoking Without Gaining Weight: The 7 + 7 Programme

PART 2: HOW TO BECOME A NON-SMOKER IN JUST SEVEN DAYS

When you complete Part 1 of the 7 + 7 Programme you will be doing exactly what it takes to prevent weight gain when you stop smoking. You will also have proved that you can make some significant changes in your life and become more like the person you want to be.

You are now ready to consider the question:

How and when do you want to stop smoking?

There are basically two ways to stop: immediately, 'cold turkey' or gradually. To stop gradually you use various methods to taper off before smoking your last cigarette. Neither way has proved to be best for everyone. So you should choose the way that is most suited to your personal style and temperament. No matter which way you choose, nicotine gum or the patch can be a great help, especially if you are a heavy smoker.

Here is a little test to see which approach to stopping is likely to be best for you.

QUIZ 3 · CHOOSING THE BEST METHOD

Answer the following questions by circling 'yes', 'no', or 'not sure'.

1. Giving up smoking is one of the most important things in the world to me right now.   yes   no   not sure

2. I know how to handle tense situations without reaching for a cigarette.   yes   no   not sure

3. I know I need to stop smoking and my reasons for stopping are strong enough for me to do it right now, this minute.   yes   no   not sure

4. If I were to stop this minute, I am confident that I would find a way to resist any future craving to smoke, even if it gets very strong.   yes   no   not sure

---

If you can answer yes to all of the questions in Quiz 3, you may be a candidate for stopping immediately, cold turkey. Before you do, however, be sure to read what I have to say in this chapter just to make sure you have all the tools you will need to be successful. Then, when you finish the chapter, set a time to stop. If not that very minute, make it tomorrow, and 'just do it'.

But supposing you are like most smokers and had some doubts?

If you are like most smokers, you felt at least a small twinge of doubt when you responded to the questions above. Like most smokers, you were not completely confident that you could resist any future craving to smoke, or that you are really capable of finding something to substitute for the gratification that cigarettes have been giving you.

In order to build the confidence you need to be a non-smoker, (1) you must develop an arsenal of weapons to handle the immediate urge to smoke each time it hits you and (2) you must develop other ways to deal with the underlying reasons that have kept you dependent on cigarettes. During the next seven days I will show you how to accomplish both tasks, so that when your quit day comes at the end of the week (or whenever you set it) you will be completely confident that you will succeed.

HOW TO DEAL WITH THE URGE TO SMOKE AT THE TIME IT HITS YOU

YOUR SHORT-DISTANCE ARTILLERY

There are several weapons to use immediately at those moments when you have the urge to reach for a cigarette. During the next seven days, you must learn and practise all of them. EVERY ONE OF THESE WEAPONS HAS A PROVEN RECORD – THEY WORK. Some people find that one is more useful than another, but most people use several in combination or at different times. After practising with these weapons for the next seven days, you will be able to choose the combination that will work best for you, and forget about the others.

The immediate urge to smoke usually lasts about five minutes before it passes. *If you can just resist reaching for a cigarette for five minutes, you shoot that urge down.* Of course, when you first stop, the urge comes back! But if you keep shooting it down, the period between urges will get longer and longer, and the urge will finally weaken and disappear. Many people think the word 'delay' when they make a decision to resist the urge, some watch the clock for five minutes, and during that time they use one or more of the following tactics.

1. Take a deep breath, hold it a moment, and exhale as if you had taken your first drag on a cigarette. This may sound paradoxical, but part of the satisfaction that you get from a cigarette is not due directly to its nicotine content, but to the body's reaction to a deep breath. By taking a deep breath you take in a maximum amount of oxygen, and when you exhale, you expel a maximum amount of carbon dioxide. The result is a feeling of relief and relaxation. Try it right now, without 'benefit' of a cigarette, and you will see what I mean. Take a full, deep breath, hold it a moment, and exhale as you might after taking the first puff of a cigarette. Notice the natural reaction of letting go in the upper part of your body, especially your shoulders. Some people like to do this several times over the five-minute period, just as if they were smoking.

2. Take a sip of water several times during this five-minute period. It lessens the desire to smoke and gives you something to do with your hands. If you

are not using nicotine replacement, it also helps to flush the nicotine from your body.

3. Put something else that's noncaloric in your mouth, such as a drinking straw, a toothpick, or, possibly the best, a piece of stick cinnamon.

4. Distract yourself. Get busy with something that will require full attention for five minutes.

5. One of the very best things you can do during this five minutes if your work normally requires sitting down is to get up and move around the entire time. Five minutes walking about, stair climbing or lifting some light weights not only helps the urge to smoke to pass, it also increases your energy level. In addition, *it burns the calories that were previously burned in response to nicotine stimulation.* Increasing activity for five minutes every hour, instead of smoking a cigarette, is an important strategy in weight-management.

6. If it does not lead to a yen for sweets, chew one piece of gum or suck one hard sweet, such as a lemon drop or mint.

7. Use nicotine replacement therapy. (More details and advice on nicotine replacement later.)

HOW TO HANDLE THE UNDERLYING REASONS FOR SMOKING

From the second quiz in Chapter 1 you became more

aware of your underlying reason or reasons for smoking. It may be for energy, to enhance pleasure and relaxation, to help cope with anxiety, anger or stress, or simply to have something to do with your hands or to fill time when you are bored. You may have become psychologically dependent on cigarettes, feeling that you cannot do without them, even without becoming chemically addicted, unless you are also a heavy smoker.

By completing Part 1 of the 7 + 7 Programme, you are already doing several things that should prove to you that you can deal with any or all of these underlying reasons for smoking. Your healthy, high-carbohydrate diet will be increasing your general energy level, as will your activity programme. In addition, your change in diet and increase in activity are stimulating your body to produce more of the same neurotransmitters and hormones that are increased with the use of nicotine, and can lead to its elimination as a necessity in your life.

Here is how to develop some specific weapons for dealing with each of the underlying reasons for smoking, together with the rationale for using them.

YOUR LONG-DISTANCE ARTILLERY

How to be a high-energy person without cigarettes. People who use cigarettes to maintain or increase their energy level have become dependent on the stimulating properties of nicotine in order to stay at, or reach, some preferred level of arousal. You become dependent on a drug's action because, whenever you use it, the body secretes certain chemicals to fight its action and return you to your natural, baseline state. Because of this regulatory reaction, you will feel below par and listless when you miss your nicotine kick. Without nicotine, your energy level can be depressed below normal until your body recovers, which may take several days or a couple of weeks. Obviously, during this period, it is especially important to do the things that can return you to your highest energy level, without the need for nicotine.

You are already doing two things that can help you feel more alive and energetic: You are eating a healthy diet and getting daily exercise. In addition, you must make sure you get enough sleep. With regard to your diet, breakfast may be particularly important. If you have been replacing breakfast with a cigarette and a cup of coffee, as many smokers do, you are much more likely to suffer weariness in the afternoon than a non-smoker who has eaten a healthy breakfast. Skipping lunch can also lead to an afternoon low.

Five minutes of just about any exercise, including walking about, stretching or lifting some light weights, is the short-term tactic that can give you an energy boost equivalent to a cigarette. Eating a carbohydrate snack can also give you an energy boost, but if sweet snacks turn on a craving for sweets, you should stick with the complex carbohydrates that I recommended in the previous chapter (low-fat crispbreads, Ryvita, rice cakes, etc.)

Finally, I want to emphasize that you cannot experience maximum energy if you are too sedentary. While a five-minute burst of activity can give you the energy boost of a cigarette, to reach your maximum energy potential you must engage the complete activity programme I outlined in the previous chapter.

How to relax and enhance the pleasure of relaxation without cigarettes. Paradoxically, nicotine affects pleasure centres of the brain that can enhance relaxation just as it can act as a stimulant and momentarily increase energy. The way in which nicotine affects you depends in part on your particular brain chemistry, and in part on the circumstances and situations in which you use cigarettes. That is, if you learned to use cigarettes in association with other relaxing behaviour, then cigarettes come to contribute to a relaxation response.

But no one needs to be dependent on cigarettes to relax. You can do a better job of relaxing by breathing deeply, as I suggested above as a weapon to defeat the immediate urge to smoke. Better still, you can learn to achieve a much greater degree of relaxation than you obtain from cigarettes by using a technique called deep muscular relaxation, or by learning to meditate. You can learn these techniques in a matter of minutes if you follow my directions in Appendix B.

Compared to the momentary relaxation you obtain from a cigarette, the state of relaxation you achieve from deep muscular relaxation or meditation can last througout the day. In fact, it's been reported that smokers who begin a practice of meditation for twenty minutes each day often find that their desire for cigarettes seems to disappear gradually. Meditation leads to a greater awareness of one's body. In contrast with the good feelings they experience with meditation, each time they smoke, meditators seem to become much more sensitive to the terrible impact that their cigarette is having on their lungs, hearts and metabolism. They begin to smoke less and less, and one day they feel ready to stop completely, and do it.

One of the best ways to minimize physical and mental tension is, once again, through daily exercise. From the physical standpoint, the muscles in your body relax much more fully after being tensed in exercise than they do without exercise. I think I can prove it to you quite quickly.

Raise your shoulders up to your ears as high as you can and hold that position for a count of five. Now release and let go. Rotate your shoulders a couple of times. Do you see how much looser they feel than before? The relaxation exercises that I will show you in Appendix B will help you deal with all kinds of momentary tension and muscular tightness. With a little practice, you will be able to turn on a relaxation response instantly.

When you combine the ability to turn on a relaxation response instantaneously with your daily activity programme, you will find yourself dealing with life in a more relaxed, self-confident fashion than you ever did as a smoker, and you will thus have dealt with this particular underlying reason for smoking.

How to deal with tension and negative affect without reaching for a cigarette. If there are many things in your life just now that are causing a great deal of tension, anxiety or frequent anger, it would be best, of course, if you could find a way to deal with the source of these emotions rather than light up a cigarette. Short of this, however, you can learn to use other tension-reducing strategies that are much healthier than smoking. And it is quite likely that if you can reduce tension in this way, you may become more effective in dealing with the stress factors in your life.

You may not realize it if smoking gives you a temporary release from tension, but cigarette smoking actually contributes to the overall tension and stress you experience from other circumstances. That's because your body becomes stressed in between nicotine-induced reactions. First, immediately after smoking, your body works hard to dispose of the nicotine contained in that cigarette. Then, when you reach some critical low point, both physical and mental tension increase as your need for a new dose of nicotine increases. You are actually more tense than you would normally be at this time, just before reaching for a cigarette, than if you never smoked at all.

As I mentioned earlier, much of the relaxing impact of smoking comes from the act of taking a deep breath itself. Try it once again, right now, without a cigarette. The more you do this, the more effective it will become. Experiment with different ways of breathing. Some people find it is more relaxing to take that deep breath, hold it for a few seconds, and exhale very slowly; others find that exhaling quickly while they focus on releasing tension in their neck and shoulders is better. But don't exhale too fast, or you may get light-headed!

The deep muscular relaxation procedure and the special breathing exercise that is included in that procedure (Appendix B) will provide both long-term and immediate tension reduction. Together with your physical activity programme, your increased feeling of well-being and self-confidence may very well help you deal with the underlying circumstances that are causing stress and tension in your life.

Dealing with psychological dependency. Although all forms of dependency on cigarettes have a certain chemical basis, unless you are a heavy smoker (a pack a day or more) the chemical basis is not likely to be particularly strong. Discomfort or annoyance when you can't smoke, such as during an aeroplane trip, or the need for a cigarette in certain social situations is mostly psychological. Over the next seven days I will give you some practice that will give you the power to eliminate psychological dependence.

Dealing with chemical dependency on nicotine. I strongly recommend that you consult your doctor about nicotine replacement therapy if you smoke a pack a day or more. While research shows that, taken by itself, nicotine replacement may not lead to significantly better success rates in remaining a non-smoker a year or two down the line, it may prove to be the critical factor in getting you through the first few days after you stop smoking. Nicotine replacement significantly reduces the extent and intensity of withdrawal reactions. In addition, it can compensate at least in part, perhaps as much as 50 per cent, for the reduction in metabolic rate and those other physiological changes that can lead to weight gain when you stop. This will give you the chance to use all the other short- and long-term weapons in the 7 + 7 Programme to fight the underlying reasons for your addiction and make sure you will be able to live happily and permanently without cigarettes in the future. See the special sections in which I discuss the use of the nicotine patch and nicotine gum, pages 93 and 94.

Keeping hands busy and fighting boredom. While it may not be the primary reason for smoking, doing something with your hands, such as lighting and handling a cigarette, can become part of a person's habitual reactions in certain situations. Some people automatically reach for a cigarette when they arrive at a party, enter a bar, make a phone call or are forced to wait for something or someone without anything else handy to engage their attention. Some people fill time with smoking when they can't think of anything else to do.

If this description applies to you, you must find different ways to replace the mechanical act of smoking. Some people find it helpful to adopt a particular behaviour that can have symbolic value; each time they do it instead of smoking they can feel positive about themselves because it means they are being successful in resisting a cigarette. Sipping water, using a toothpick or a straw in place of a cigarette, working on the crossword puzzle in the newspaper, knitting or fingering a special coin or medallion can come to represent and symbolize your determination not to smoke.

If boredom is sometimes an issue for you, consider whether giving up smoking could be a time when you start on a hobby or a vocation that you have always wanted to pursue, or which you have been neglecting. It would be great if smoking didn't go well with such an activity! Perhaps working on a puzzle, knitting or playing a computer game could become an interesting, relaxing way to fill otherwise empty time.

THE SEVEN-DAY PROGRAMME TO STOP SMOKING

NICOTINE INTERACTS WITH MANY OTHER DRUGS. IF YOU ARE TAKING ANY PRESCRIPTION OR OVER-THE-COUNTER MEDICATION, BE SURE TO INFORM YOUR DOCTOR THAT YOU ARE ABOUT TO STOP SMOKING.

The first thing you must do to set the actual process of giving up in motion is to set an official quit date. While you can be flexible, depending on how you feel during the next seven days, I recommend one week from today. Seven days will give you all the time you need to practise with your anti-smoking weaponry and to demonstrate to yourself that you can be a successful quitter. One the eighth day, it's all systems go.

Days 1 and 2

Monitor your smoking behaviour for two days. Each time you smoke, ask yourself this short set of questions:

1. Why am I smoking this cigarette?
2. If I chose to, would this be an easy one or a difficult one to do without?
3. If I decided not to smoke this particular cigarette, what would I do instead?

Although many people who stop on their own just make mental notes of the time, place and reasons for smoking, and begin to plan how they will deal with each situation, you are likely to be more successful if you keep a written record. Use the Smoking Record at the end of this chapter.

It's best to keep your record as you smoke each cigarette, since that will force you to review all the suggestions I have made, and plan carefully. However, if this is inconvenient, take time at the end of the day to review your smoking behaviour again. Recall as many of the situations in which you smoked, and think seriously about your plans for dealing with each.[1]

[1] Some people find it helpful to wrap a piece of notepaper around their pack of cigarettes and fasten it with tape. They keep their smoking record on this piece of paper.

If you have been smoking as a way to cope with stress or negative emotions, be sure to practise the relaxation or meditation techniques in Appendix B each day.

Day 3

It's time to test and hone your weapons. Use your short-range artillery to shoot down the urge to smoke *at least once today*. Start with a cigarette that you rated 'easy' during the two-day monitoring period, and do it at a time when you can test out as many of your weapons as possible. During the five minute period that it will take for the urge to smoke to pass, try out one, or better several, of the following weapons until you find your own best combination:

1. Take a deep breath as though smoking, and repeat as necessary.
2. Sip water.
3. Suck on a straw, toothpick or stick of cinnamon.
4. Eat ONE hard sweet or chew ONE piece of gum.
5. Distract yourself – get busy with something that requires five minutes of your undivided attention.
6. Get up and walk about or lift light weights.
7. Try out a piece of nicotine gum, if you have decided to use nicotine replacement therapy.

Begin to develop this attitude: 'If I can skip one ciga-rette, I can skip them all.' And you *will* be able to skip them all as you continue to hone the use of your weapons over the next few days.

You can, of course, decide to skip more than one

cigarette today, and it will get easier and easier if you think of it only as a game, something like one of those arcade or computer games in which you shoot down evil monsters. Only, in this case, the evil monsters are cigarettes.

As in those arcade or computer games, it can take a while until you master the strategy and tactics to win. So if you fail in any given effort to skip a cigarette, just go back to your war room and replot your strategy.

If all of this comes easy to you, just keep track of your progress mentally. Every success is a victory over a powerful drug. However, I think you will find it helpful to continue to keep a record of your smoking behaviour today and for the rest of the week as you did the first two days. The record will help you plan your future course of action in each of the situations in which you smoke.

Be sure to continue to practise relaxation or meditation each day if you are using one of these strategies to deal with your underlying reasons for smoking.

Day 4

Today is another test day. If you haven't already jumped the gun and tried it on Day 3, it's time to skip *at least one cigarette* that you rated 'difficult' during your two-day monitoring period.

Keep your Smoking Record and if you fail in your effort to skip a difficult cigarette don't be too hard on yourself. This is a practice period and you are experimenting with your various weapons in order to learn how to be effective.

If in fact you found skipping that cigarette very

difficult, or, indeed, you failed in the end, review carefully everything that got in the way of your being successful. The most common things that lead to difficulty or failure, together with some possible remedies, include:

The chemical aspects of addiction: When you skip cigarettes you feel lousy! *Remedy:* If you are a heavy smoker, once again I encourage you to use nicotine replacement therapy if you have not already decided to do so.

Social pressure: You found yourself in a situation in which you and your friends are engaging in an activity (cocktail party, coffee break) during which you normally smoke. *Remedy:* Tell everyone who might have a negative impact on your desire to stop smoking of your serious intentions *and why it is important to you.* If they are really your friends, and even if they are smokers themselves, they will avoid doing anything that might encourage you to join them. You may also find it helpful to enlist a special non-smoking friend for social support, someone with whom you can talk things over during this quitting period. Just be sure you tell this person what might be helpful to you and what might not, since even with the best intentions your friend may say or do things that just make the situation worse. Finally, in this regard, you must ask yourself, 'If I continue to face this kind of social situation, will I really be able to stop? Do I need to avoid such situations for a certain period of time, until I become fully confident that I can be a non-smoker for ever?' If you feel that you will not be able to resist the social pressure to smoke, and you are serious about stopping, you must avoid such situations for about two or three weeks, until the urge to smoke is gone.

Extreme tension or negative emotion: Something beyond the usually ordinary stress of daily living, a crisis, occurs in your work or personal life, and one of your underlying reasons for smoking has been for tension reduction or relaxation. *Remedy:* This may require a combination of remedies. First, as a basis for dealing with negative emotions, redouble your efforts to use the tension-reduction weapons I have already given you. Get away from the particular environment with which the tension is directly associated – go to another room or take a walk. Use your relaxation strategy. Second, you may find that nicotine replacement therapy in the form of the gum, which has some of the same cyclic effect of cigarettes, provides enough tension relief to get you through your immediate reaction. Third, talk over your problems with a sympathetic listener. It's better to blow off steam than to inhale cigarette smoke. Start with a friend or relation with whom you have a good relationship. If that doesn't help, phone the Smokers Quitline (see Appendix D) or you could think about discussing the problem with your minister, priest or rabbi. Finally if you really cannot find a way to deal with the stress factors in your life, except as a smoker, these factors are probably serious enough for you to seek professional help or consult one of the specialist agencies such as the Samaritans or Relate.

Days 5, 6 and 7

This is the home stretch.

Your main objective in these next three days is to end up on Day 7 smoking about half the number of cigarettes you used to smoke before you began Part 2 of the

7 + 7 Programme. If you used to smoke a full pack, aim for about ten cigarettes on Day 7.[1] Fewer is even better.

In order to reach your objective for Day 7, set a target for Days 5 and 6, cutting out a few cigarettes each day in a way that will move you gradually toward your goal. This attenuation permits a gradual withdrawal from nicotine and should make quitting easier. Maintain your Smoking Record during these three days and keep practising with the tactics that seem most helpful to you.

At some point during these three days you may feel like jumping the gun and stopping before your official quit date. You're the boss and the moment you feel confident that you can succeed, 'just do it'.

But supposing you still have doubts?

If this occurs, the underlying reason in all likelihood is your dependence on the chemical impact of nicotine. It's a very powerful drug, and many forces have been operating to make you addicted. Since you have come this far, I urge you once again to discuss immediately with your doctor the use of nicotine replacement therapy. It can significantly reduce withdrawal symptoms and can get you over the hump. Remember, nicotine itself is not carcinogenic. It's the hook that has got you to smoke cigarettes, which carry numerous other substances that are dangerous to your health. With the help

---

[1] If you normally smoke a high- or medium-nicotine brand of cigarettes, some experts suggest that you switch to a brand one step lower in nicotine content as a way to cut your nicotine intake prior to giving up completely. Or you might try switching from regular to menthol, or vice versa, to make cigarettes less attractive in flavour. The problem with this approach is that it maintains the habit aspects of smoking in the many situations in which you may smoke, and, in addition, can lead to inhaling more deeply or more often with each cigarette in order to maximize your nicotine intake.

of either the patch or nicotine gum, you will have all the other weapons you need from the 7 + 7 Programme to be a successful quitter.

THE NICOTINE PATCH

Your doctor or pharmacist will give you advice on how to use the patch. Normally, a heavy smoker might use it for up to six weeks, starting first with a patch that contains a high dose of nicotine. The nicotine is released slowly throughout the day and the nicotine content of your bloodstream tends to be about 50 per cent of what it might be if you continued to smoke. Every two weeks, the dose is reduced. Typically, heavy smokers start with a 21-milligram patch, reduce it to 14 milligrams after two weeks, and then finish up with a 7-milligram patch. DO NOT SMOKE while you are using the patch or you may experience a dangerous overdose of nicotine.

The patch may be most useful for smokers who start early in the day and continue on a fairly regular basis, since it releases nicotine on a continual, gradual basis. If you tend to concentrate your smoking at one particular time every day, say at night, and only smoke lightly if at all during the rest of the day, a continuous release of nicotine may cause discomfort (dizziness or headaches) during the time when you are not accustomed to smoking very much. The gum would be more suitable in these circumstances. Also, a small percentage of users suffer from local irritation or itchiness from the patch.

HOW TO USE NICOTINE GUM

When you use nicotine gum, chewing a piece every hour or whenever you have the urge to smoke, you tend to mimic the cyclic rise and fall of nicotine in your system that occurs when you smoke cigarettes. I was impressed by the impact of the gum when I tried it. I felt the same kind of 'hit' that I used to get from cigarettes. Of course, I'm no longer a smoker, so the magnitude of the effect was more like the one you get from a cigarette after not smoking for a day or two.

The gum comes in 2- or 4-milligram doses and is available without a doctor's prescription. Normally, the higher dose is recommended only for heavy smokers when they first stop smoking, and is then reduced.

You can use up to thirty pieces of the 2-milligram gum a day, although most people average between twelve and sixteen. The upper limit for the 4-milligram gum is twenty pieces, and the average is ten. Because of the danger of remaining addicted to nicotine and the greater likelihood of side effects (discussed below), many experts shy away from recommending the 4-milligram gum, and I, too, suggest you use the 2-milligram gum, unless your doctor recommends otherwise.

If you use the gum, use it to the extent it can be helpful in combination with certain of your other anti-smoking weapons. Take a deep breath, or walk around for five minutes (but do not drink liquid while the gum is in your mouth because it will reduce its effectiveness and possibly upset your stomach). You can use the 2-milligram gum each time you feel the urge to smoke, or to a timetable such as every hour if you are not a particularly heavy smoker (it will help to minimize withdrawal symptoms).

Although some experts suggest you wait until quit day to begin using the gum, I think you will do better if you begin to experiment and get used to using it during Part 2 of the 7 + 7 Programme. Substitute a piece of gum for one or two *(but not more)* of the cigarettes that you are beginning to omit each day. The reasons for substituting gum for only one or two cigarettes during this period, and not for all of them, are to make sure you don't overdose yourself on nicotine and also to make sure that the amount of nicotine that's present in your system when you stop has been lowered.

Here are specific instructions for maximizing the effectiveness of nicotine gum (in the 2-milligram dose).

WHEN TO USE

Chew a piece each time you feel the urge to smoke.

Wait at least fifteen minutes after drinking coffee, tea, milk, fruit juices or cola beverages before using the gum. The acid in the drinks reduces its effectiveness.

If the taste of the gum is not offensive first thing in the morning, you can start chewing as soon as you wake, including first thing in the morning on quit day.

HOW TO USE

Chew the gum very slowly until you taste it. Chew just once or twice and wait a moment to see if the taste becomes evident. If not, chew again.

When the taste appears, place the nicotine gum between your cheek and your gum line.

After the flavour disappears, take a chew or two until

you taste it again, and put the gum back in your cheek. This should occur every minute or two.

Chew each piece of gum for not less than twenty and up to thirty minutes, then throw it away.

Do not drink any liquids while the gum is in your mouth.

HOW MUCH TO USE

Use ten to thirty pieces of gum each day.

Do not use more than thirty pieces a day.

As the urge to smoke eases, gradually reduce the number of pieces used each day.

However, do not underuse the gum during the first week of stopping if you sense any significant withdrawal symptoms, especially cigarette cravings. Correct use significantly reduces withdrawal symptoms.

Most people can be finished with the gum in a month or less, but you can continue to use it for up to six months.

SIDE EFFECTS

Some people experience a sore jaw, irritation of the mouth, heartburn, nausea or hiccups. These can usually be prevented by chewing the gum more slowly. Some people object to the taste of the gum itself when they chew for a full half hour. If this occurs in your case, try chewing for only twenty-five minutes (not less than twenty minutes for a reasonably full impact) and on a schedule of once an hour. Resist any urge to smoke between pieces of gum with one of your other smoke-resisting weapons.

WARNING: Pregnant or lactating women should not use the gum. Smokers with any form of heart disease should use the gum only on the advice and under the close supervision of their doctor.

SPECIAL ADVICE FOR QUIT DAY

Unless you are completely confident that the presence and sight of a cigarette will not provide a stimulus to smoke, I think you should get rid of all smoking paraphernalia, at least temporarily. Throw away or give away all cigarettes, ashtrays, cigarette lighters and matches in your home and workplace. There is no need to force yourself to resist temptation that is staring you in the face. Almost every ex-smoker that I have spoken to has told me that they failed to give up when they kept cigarettes in their home or office. They usually persuaded themselves that 'just this one' would not hurt. But it did. Once you are a confident non-smoker you may be able to have cigarettes around without danger of relapsing, but then, why would you want to?

In spite of all your excellent preparation you may still experience some withdrawal symptoms. Be prepared. They may last only a day or two, or as long as two to four weeks.

The 7 + 7 Programme will have prepared you to deal with changes in appetite and the craving for cigarettes that smokers face when they stop. Here are some ways to cope with the other typical withdrawal symptoms.

Dizziness may occur during the first day or two. It may last a few moments at a time. Take a rest – it will pass.

Headaches may occur at any time during the first few weeks. Relax, take your usual headache medication, try a cold compress on the back of your neck. Slight tension headaches can sometimes be relieved by going for a walk.

Tiredness can occur during the first two to four weeks, but is not likely if you maintain your exercise programme, take time for a relaxation or meditation period once or twice a day, and get enough sleep.

Coughing may actually increase for a day or two after stopping, as your lungs get rid of the smoking residue that coats them. The cough will disappear gradually over several days. It helps to sip water or suck a cough drop or boiled sweet.

Tightness in the chest may occur during the first week. Take a rest and breathe deeply – it will pass.

Trouble sleeping may occur the first few nights. Do not drink caffeinated beverages late in the day; do not do strenuous or prolonged physical activity during the two hours before going to sleep; drink a glass of milk or eat a bowl of cereal with milk as your night-time snack, and take a hot bath before retiring.

Constipation may occur during the first two to four weeks after stopping, but is not likely if you are following the nutrition advice in Part 1 of the 7 + 7 Programme. Eating a high-fibre diet (fruits, vegetables and grain foods), drinking plenty of water and getting at least forty-five minutes of physical activity each day are your best safeguards.

Difficulty concentrating may occur during the first few weeks. Be prepared for this; take a break and do something physical for a few minutes.

OTHER PHARMACOLOGICAL AIDS TO SMOKING CESSATION AND WEIGHT MANAGEMENT

Depending upon your needs, there are a number of other pharmacological aids that your doctor may recommend to help minimize withdrawal symptoms and manage your weight. Some are available without a prescription, but should not be used when you stop smoking without consulting your doctor. These include:

1. Fenfluramine. This prescription drug stimulates serotonin secretion to control appetite and sweet cravings, and has a tendency to increase your metabolic rate.
2. Phenylpropanolamine. This drug, found in prescription and over-the-counter weight-management and cold symptom medications, may have an appetite-suppressing effect.
3. Other appetite suppressants that might be prescribed by your doctor for a brief period include benzphetamine, diethylpropion, mazindol, phendimetrazine, phenmetrazine and phentermine. These drugs lose their effectiveness in a short time and occasionally cause serous side effects. They should be monitored by your doctor.
4. The amino acid tryptophan may also have an appetite-suppressing effect since it increases the activity of serotonin. One study reported an effective dosage of 50 milligrams per kilogram of body weight daily.
5. Some people, typically heavy smokers, feel

depressed when they stop smoking. Prozac, while not appearing to have any effect on weight, has been found useful in preventing serious depression.

A WORD ABOUT CAFFEINE AND ALCOHOL

Since nicotine is a central nervous system stimulant, you may be wondering if you could substitute caffeine for nicotine. *Don't do it.*

If you customarily drink several cups of coffee, tea or other beverages containing caffeine, BE VERY CAREFUL NOT TO INCREASE YOUR CONSUMPTION! Nicotine suppresses the effect of caffeine, cutting some of its stimulating properties by half or even a little more. So, when you stop smoking, the impact of caffeine increases. If you drink more than a couple of cups of coffee, tea or other caffeinated beverages every day, and continue to do so after you stop smoking, you may actually find youself getting jittery so that you have to cut back. (Unfortunately, in spite of an increase in the impact of caffeine on your nerves when you stop smoking, it does not seem to compensate for the metabolic changes that occur which cause weight gain.)

If, however, as a smoker you have not been drinking beverages containing caffeine, you might consult your doctor about using prescription or over-the-counter caffeine tablets. As someone who has not previously used caffeine, there is some possiblity that it could have a stimulating effect on your metabolic rate. But I would not advise anyone to develop a caffeine habit to replace the nicotine habit. Caffeine can also cause some undesirable side effects, such as nervousness, diarrhoea, dizziness, fast heartbeat and trouble sleeping. And if you start to drink coffee as a way to obtain caffeine, you may end up with an acid stomach and heartburn.

Alcohol, in contrast with nicotine and caffeine, has a sedating effect. If you smoke when you drink, the stimulating properties of nicotine can counter, to a certain extent, the sedating effects of alcohol. When you stop smoking the sedating or intoxicating impact of alcohol will therefore increase. If you consume more than a modest amount of alcohol, you should cut back. *Alcohol should always be used in moderation by people concerned about their weight.* While the mechanism is not completely understood, alcohol facilitates fat storage. As a former smoker and someone interested in managing your weight, you should restrict your intake to one or two glasses of wine, or the equivalent, per day.

And now, CONGRATULATIONS!

You have finished the 7 + 7 Programme of *How to Stop Smoking Without Gaining Weight*. I want to wish you good luck in your efforts to remain a non-smoker and good health in the years to come.

If, in the future, you experience any difficulty managing your weight using the general nutrition advice I have given you in Part 1 of the 7 + 7 Programme and the diet you have designed for yourself based on this advice, go directly to the next chapter and follow the explicit daily menu plan in the Ex-Smoker's Weight-Management Programme.

SOME WORDS OF ADVICE AND ENCOURAGEMENT FROM EX-SMOKERS

During the months in which I was writing this book I interviewed a number of ex-smokers, asking them what the key factors were in motivating them to stop smoking, and what strategies they used to prevent weight gain as well as to help them to stop.

Karen Ashworth, an executive with a public relations firm, expressed well the common fears and wishes that we all experienced as smokers and which motivated us to stop. 'I watched my father go in and out of the hospital. He has emphysema and suffers repeatedly from pneumonia. He can hardly breathe sometimes, and walking even a short distance is nearly impossible. He has to give himself breathing treatments every four hours with his portable breathing machine. He keeps saying to me, 'If I only knew what I know now thirty years ago.' Well, I know it and I quit last year on July 5th, at the very age my father would have been if he had quit thirty years ago.'

When I asked Karen what she did to maintain her weight, besides mentioning the low-fat alternatives she was taking, Karen said, 'Drinking water was most important when I quit. I carried a half-gallon flask to work, and sipped every time I thought about smoking when I first quit, but then I discovered it was the best thing to do to keep from eating unnecessarily, too. I still carry a flask every day.' As for exercise, in addition to using every opportunity to move around during the working day, Karen told me, 'I do about thirty minutes a day. I alternate between step aerobics [she has a videotape], an exercise bicycle, and a stair climber. But I'm always fighting five extra pounds.' I think it's going to take a little more physical activity to take care of anyone's last five pounds, but I think you can consider yourself successful if you, too, can do as well as Karen.

In my own case, I stopped smoking cigarettes

habitually in 1953 when the research I had been studying convinced me that cigarettes caused cancer. But I switched to cigars and continued to smoke them, one or two a day, as well as a cigarette perhaps once a month, until one day in the spring of 1983. As I was cleaning the cigar-smoke film that coated the inside windshield of my car, I suddenly became very conscious that that same film was coating my lungs even though I was not inhaling cigar smoke directly. It was on my mind when I was talking with my wife in our den and reached for a cigar later that same day. At that moment the thought occurred to me that I was killing her with cigar smoke, as well as myself. I did not light that cigar, and have never lit one since. After about two days, I did not miss smoking at all, and it was certainly motivating to see the cough that I had developed begin to disappear. Since I was already a very active person, playing competitive tennis several times a week and jogging about 25 miles a week, I did not regain any of the 70 pounds (32 kilos) I had previously lost in 1963.

My literary agent, Richard Pine, stopped smoking seventeen years ago, at the age of twenty-two. When I asked him what motivated him he told me, 'I tried to quit a few times in college, but failed. I had a smoker's cough, which reminded me all was not completely well inside my chest, but I began to smoke more right after college. A little more than a pack a day became two-plus and I began experiencing side effects I didn't like: losing a step or two on the basketball court and a thickening of my saliva. They bothered me an awful lot. I thought of quitting every morning and began to have nightmares of falling asleep with a cigarette in my hand. Over the course of a few months I became absolutely certain that I was well on the road to emphysema or cancer. I had visions of myself lying in the hospital, unconscious and connected to a jungle of tubes and machines that barely kept me alive. So, I came to the point where I knew I had to make a choice: keep smoking and die a painful, ugly death some time in the near future, or quit and live a long life.' Richard was always thin and never did overeat, and being very active – walking a lot, riding a bicycle, and playing basketball – he never gained weight when he stopped. And he is just as slim today as the day I met him in the summer of 1981.

In spite of being a smoker, Ben Wilson, who is a minister at one of our local churches, had never been able to manage his weight. He was fifty-two years old and weighed over 18 stone (116 kilos) when the need to make what had become an annual trip to the tailor to alter his clothes finally convinced him it was time to change. It was on his way home from the tailor that day, in December 1991, with his newly enlarged wardrobe, that he decided to follow *The T-Factor Diet*, which he had heard about, but never used. I talked with him about his weight and smoking experiences on 2 February 1994, a few days after one of his parishioners told me about his success story.

'The first thing I did when I got home that day [in 1991] was throw out the candy and the colas that I knew were contributing to my problem. I didn't want them around the house to tempt me. I had also been cooking up a batch of fried fish or chicken about three times a week. Now I bake or broil, but I don't deny myself completely. Occasionally I do indulge in a hamburger, but it's not very often.'

Because his ever-increasing weight was contributing

to the deterioration of his knee joints, and he was ultimately going to need surgery, Ben's doctor advised him that he should not attempt a vigorous aerobic programme that might cause further damage, but that he should focus on strength training for his upper body and include the leg exercises that would be important for rehabilitation after surgery. However, short periods of walking at a moderate pace were just fine, so, to burn calories, his doctor advised him to simply walk whenever he could throughout the day. Ben said, 'I rarely sit still for any length of time – I use every excuse to walk.'

Ben decided to stop smoking about one year later, after he had lost over 50 pounds (23 kilos). 'I weighed about 205 pounds [15 stone/92 kilos] when I quit smoking and I decided to use the nicotine patch to help me with the urge to smoke and maybe my weight. But I already knew what I needed to do [for my weight] – stick to a low-fat diet and keep exercising, so I quit using the patches after fourteen days.' Fortunately, Ben's strength-training programme, which he does for thirty-five minutes three times a week at a fitness centre, his wake-up routine which includes 100 stomach crunches every morning, and his walking about whenever he finds a chance throughout the day seem to be just the right balance of physical activity, since this combination of exercise increases the burning of both fat and glucose in his fuel mixture.

'I continued to lose weight after I quit smoking by following *The T-Factor Diet* and keeping up with my exercise. With *The T-Factor Diet* I already had my appetite under control and it never became a problem. But someone told me to drink a lot of water after I quit smoking and I think that helped flush the nicotine out of my system and reduced my desire to smoke. I lost another 25 pounds [11 kilos] after I quit smoking and my weight stays now between 178 and 180 pounds [about 12½ stone/80–81 kilos].'

Ben told me that he has no trouble maintaining his weight, so I congratulated him again and wished him continued success. He quickly responded to my good wishes with, 'You don't need to worry. I work at this. I *mean* to do it, I mean to succeed.' I wish you could have heard the calm determination in his voice as he made these last remarks.

Harry Gillis is sixty-eight years old and recently retired from his position as a vice-president at a bank in Nashville. 'I'd been a pack-a-day smoker for forty years, and had made many efforts to stop, but it never lasted too long. Finally, I enrolled in a smoking-cessation clinic at a local hospital in July 1990. This time I made up my mind to quit. I think that's necessary – you really have to make up your mind to quit.'

I asked Harry to give me some details about the pro-gramme and he said, 'As part of the programme we had to record the time, place and reason why we were smoking each cigarette. It was such a terrible bother that I just quit, cold turkey, without waiting for the group's quit date. I've never smoked since. The thing that helped me most was the group support. I was get-ting a divorce at the time, and without the group's influence I think the stress would have driven me back to cigarettes. When I went to a follow-up meeting in February 1991, several of the others had started smok-ing again. They thought they could have just one now and then, and pretty soon they were back on cigarettes. I don't think you can do that. At least I don't think I could, so I never have. I don't keep any stuff around the house, either, but I have one friend who has kept his last pack of cigarettes in his freezer for ten years, and never smoked. Pretty amazing. I think.'

When I asked Harry about his weight, he told me, 'Exercise made the big difference for me. During the programme I exercised for two hours a day and lost 25 pounds [2 stone/11 kilos]. Five times a week I would go to the fitness centre at the hospital and I walked on those days, too. Now I just walk for 4 miles every morning.'

I could go on with many such stories, each a bit different, but all will share one central, common feature – the need for exercise if you want to manage your weight. The last story puts it very well, and was told to me by Bob Billings, a Nashville lawyer. 'I had tried for many years to quit smoking before I was finally successful in February 1992. And, in spite of being a smoker, my weight had also fluctuated, up and down, as much as 25 pounds [2 stone/11 kilos]. This time, when I quit, I had my exercise programme firmly in place.[1] I had joined the exercise programme at the Dyani Center in the fall of 1991, and I was going three or four times a week. To make sure I was active every day, I bought a Nordic Track for the home. When I decided to quit smoking I had already lost 7 pounds and I was feeling pretty good about myself because I was exercising. I used the patch when I quit smoking and the patch made me feel even better. I used it for six weeks, starting with a 21-milligram patch for two

[1] Bob was the first person to use the expression 'firmly in place' about his exercise programme. I liked it so well that I used it myself elsewhere in this book.

weeks, 14 milligrams for the next two weeks, and ending with 7 milligrams. I'm now another 12 pounds [5.4 kilos] lighter and I have been off cigarettes for a year.'

SMOKING RECORD

Instructions. Use the top section of each page to record cigarettes actually smoked during each of the next seven days. Record the time, place and with whom, reason, whether it will be an easy (E) or difficult (D) cigarette to eliminate, and the anti-smoking weapon or weapons you plan to use to eliminate that cigarette. *Use the bottom section* of each page as you begin to eliminate cigarettes, beginning on Day 3. Record the time and other information each time you make a decision to eliminate a particular cigarette. Indicate what anti-smoking weapon you employed. In the comments section indicate whether or not you were successful, and the reason why in either case. In case of failure, plan what you will do next time.

Seven-day
Smoking Record
Charts

DAY 1 – CIGARETTES SMOKED

Date:

No.	Time	Place & with whom	Reason for smoking	E or D	Weapon to use
1					
2					
3					
4					
5					
6					
7					
8					
9					
10					
11					
12					
13					
14					
15					
16					
17					
18					
19					
20					

No.	Time	Place & with whom	Reason for smoking	E or D	Weapon to use
21					
22					
23					
24					
25					
26					
27					
28					
29					
30					
31					
32					
33					
34					
35					
36					
37					
38					
39					
40					

DAY 2 – CIGARETTES SMOKED

Date:

No.	Time	Place & with whom	Reason for smoking	E or D	Weapon to use
1					
2					
3					
4					
5					
6					
7					
8					
9					
10					
11					
12					
13					
14					
15					
16					
17					
18					
19					
20					

No.	Time	Place & with whom	Reason for smoking	E or D	Weapon to use
21					
22					
23					
24					
25					
26					
27					
28					
29					
30					
31					
32					
33					
34					
35					
36					
37					
38					
39					
40					

DAY 3 – CIGARETTES SMOKED

Date:

No.	Time	Place & with whom	Reason for smoking	E or D	Weapon to use
1					
2					
3					
4					
5					
6					
7					
8					
9					
10					
11					
12					
13					
14					
15					
16					
17					
18					
19					
20					
21					
22					

No.	Time	Place & with whom	Reason for smoking	E or D	Weapon to use
23					
24					
25					
26					
27					
28					
29					
30					
31					
32					
33					
34					
35					
36					
37					
38					

CIGARETTES ELIMINATED

No.	Time	Place & with whom	Weapon(s) used	E or D	Comments
1					
2					
3					
4					
5					

DAY 4 – CIGARETTES SMOKED

Date:

No.	Time	Place & with whom	Reason for smoking	E or D	Weapon to use
1					
2					
3					
4					
5					
6					
7					
8					
9					
10					
11					
12					
13					
14					
15					
16					
17					
18					
19					
20					
21					
22					
23					

No.	Time	Place & with whom	Reason for smoking	E or D	Weapon to use
24					
25					
26					
27					
28					
29					
30					
31					
32					
33					
34					
35					

CIGARETTES ELIMINATED

No.	Time	Place & with whom	Weapon(s) used	E or D	Comments
1					
2					
3					
4					
5					
6					
7					
8					
9					
10					

117

DAY 5 – CIGARETTES SMOKED

Date:

No.	Time	Place & with whom	Reason for smoking	E or D	Weapon to use
1					
2					
3					
4					
5					
6					
7					
8					
9					
10					
11					
12					
13					
14					
15					
16					
17					
18					
19					
20					

No.	Time	Place & with whom	Reason for smoking	E or D	Weapon to use
21					
22					
23					
24					
25					
26					
27					
28					
29					
30					

CIGARETTES ELIMINATED

No.	Time	Place & with whom	Weapon(s) used	E or D	Comments
1					
2					
3					
4					
5					
6					
7					
8					
9					
10					

DAY 6 – CIGARETTES SMOKED

Date:

No.	Time	Place & with whom	Reason for smoking	E or D	Weapon to use
1					
2					
3					
4					
5					
6					
7					
8					
9					
10					
11					
12					
13					
14					
15					
16					
17					
18					
19					
20					

No.	Time	Place & with whom	Reason for smoking	E or D	Weapon to use
21					
22					
23					
24					
25					

CIGARETTES ELIMINATED

No.	Time	Place & with whom	Weapon(s) used	E or D	Comments
1					
2					
3					
4					
5					
6					
7					
8					
9					
10					
11					
12					
13					
14					
15					

DAY 7 – CIGARETTES SMOKED

Date:

No.	Time	Place & with whom	Reason for smoking	E or D	Weapon to use
1					
2					
3					
4					
5					
6					
7					
8					
9					
10					
11					
12					
13					
14					
15					
16					
17					
18					
19					
20					

CIGARETTES ELIMINATED

No.	Time	Place & with whom	Weapon(s) used	E or D	Comments
1					
2					
3					
4					
5					
6					
7					
8					
9					
10					
11					
12					
13					
14					
15					
16					
17					
18					
19					
20					

5

The Ex-Smoker's Weight-Management Programme

If you are a former smoker who's gained weight after stopping, don't despair. You'll be able to lose it quite painlessly by following the advice in this chapter.

Former smokers who have been off cigarettes long enough to feel confident that they are in no danger of relapsing can begin immediately with the Ex-Smoker's Weight-Management Programme on page 127.

But supposing you have just recently given up, still crave cigarettes and, to top it off, find that you are gaining weight?

If you have just recently stopped and are still fighting the urge to resume smoking, it's best to move gradually into a weight-management programme. Trying to change your dietary habits too quickly can add to the stress you may still be experiencing in your efforts to remain a non-smoker and only increase your craving for cigarettes. Your highest priority at this time should be *to remain a non-smoker*.

Aim first to stop gaining weight, and once you've accomplished that, think about what additional steps it will take to lose weight. The best way to do this without impairing your ability to remain a non-smoker is to use the following strategy.

1. Increase your physical activity. This is more important in the total picture right now than changing your diet because the more active you become, the easier it will be to remain a non-smoker as well as to manage your weight. Review my advice on pages 66–70 and set a target of at least forty-five minutes a day.

2. Then begin to cut the fat in your diet. Start by making low-fat substitutions for the high-fat foods in accordance with my meal and snack suggestions in Chapter 3. Keep track of your daily fat-gram intake. Move gradually toward the daily fat-gram target in the Ex-Smoker's Weight-Management Programme described below. If you are able, in time, to reach the target level for weight loss comfortably, without endangering your ability to remain a non-smoker, you should begin to lose weight.

3. If increasing your activity and cutting the fat as I recommend do not prevent further weight gain and start you on the road to losing weight, as it will in almost all cases, you may be consuming too many carbohydrates. Monitor your carbohydrate intake to determine whether you are eating too many sweet things independently of fat, that is, eating

more than one boiled sweet or hard mint instead of smoking a cigarette, or more than one serving of complex carbohydrates at snack times. Study my advice on carbohydrate foods in Chapter 3. You'll find some other suggestions below.

4. Discuss with your doctor the use of nicotine replacement, with the patch or gum, or use of one of the pharmacological aids to smoking cessation and weight control I discussed on pages 93–100. These aids serve a dual purpose since, like increasing physical activity, they work simultaneously to ensure your success in remaining a non-smoker and in managing your weight.

5. Continue to use whatever smoking-cessation strategies are helping you to deal with your desire to smoke until you are safely through the transition to becoming a fully successful non-smoker. Then begin the Ex-Smoker's Weight-Management Programme, which contains detailed daily menus and a daily fat-gram target that will help you gradually and permanently lose whatever weight you have gained.

THE EX-SMOKER'S WEIGHT-MANAGEMENT PROGRAMME

The amount of fat on your body is adjusted primarily by the amount of fat in your diet.

If you increase or decrease the amount of fat in your diet, you gain or lose a certain percentage of fat from your body. Each of us has a certain range over which this occurs rather easily. It's genetically determined. For the rare person with really skinny genes, perhaps one in twenty, the range may be only a few pounds either way no matter how much fat that person eats. But for most of us, the range is more like 20 to 50 pounds (9 to 23 kilos). And for those of us with a strong genetic tendency towards obesity, it can be 7 stone (45 kilos) or even more in extreme cases.

Of course, physical activity narrows the range. An ultra-marathon runner, who runs 50- or 100-mile races several times a year, and who runs over 10 miles a day in training, will tend to burn off whatever fat he eats before it can settle in his fat cells. But at lesser daily energy expenditures, say even 5 miles of jogging, people are still susceptible to 20-pound (9-kilo) variations, or even more, as a function of the amount of fat in their diets.

About 95 per cent of the people who have any weight to lose will lose it by cutting the fat in their diets to the following levels:

Women	20 to 40 grams a day
Men	30 to 60 grams a day

And, if they are in a sedentary occupation, they'll lose weight by increasing physical activity to the tune of between 200 and 300 calories of extra energy expenditure every day. This can be accomplished with about forty-five to sixty minutes of brisk walking, or any other equivalent exercise.

What about the other 5 per cent for whom this nice combination of sound nutrition and exercise doesn't work? And supposing that 5 per cent includes you!

Then, in all likelihood, your carbohydrate intake is more than your particular metabolism can burn off, in spite of a healthy amount of physical activity and a low-fat diet. But let's start by assuming you fit in with the majority because the way to deal with your diet in this case is quite simple and painless. There is no need to take drastic steps until they prove to be necessary. If, unfortunately, you find that the simple approach is not effective, I'll show you what additional steps you need to take later in this chapter.

It's essential that you put my recommendations for physical activity into practice. Go all the way! Although it's possible for most people to lose a significant amount of weight just by cutting the fat in their diets to between 20 and 25 per cent of total calories, with only a small increase in activity, my experience is that they get about halfway to the weight they'd like to be and hit a plateau. That is all the adjustment that their bodies will make to a 20 to 25 per cent fat diet if they remain sedentary. They are stuck there. To lose any more weight without adding forty-five to sixty minutes a day of activity can require cutting fat to as low as 10 per cent of total calories.

A healthy diet with only 10 per cent of calories from fat can be designed, and all overweight people who do not suffer from a serious genetic defect will, in time, lose all their surplus body fat and become quite thin if they eat no more than 10 per cent of their calories from fat. In addition, in some cases a diet this low in fat can stop the progression of atherosclerosis and possibly lead to a small reversal in people who suffer from this disease. Most people, however, will find such a spartan diet a great bother to prepare and almost impossible to live with. Very few can remain motivated to do so, even in the presence of a life-threatening illness.[1]

[1] There are actually some people with a rare from of hyperlipidemia (elevated triglycerides in their bloodstream) who cannot tolerate a diet this low in fat together with 70 to 80 per cent of calories from carbohydrates. You should not undertake this extreme form of diet without consulting your doctor.

But, as you will see below, it is very easy to design and prepare a palatable diet that contains between 20 and 25 per cent of calories from fat. Together with the physical activity I recommend, almost all people will lose weight on such a diet. The low end of the target ranges that I suggest (20–40 grams of fat per day for women, 30–60 grams of fat for men) will tend to bring your diet down to around the 20 per cent level in calories from fat, and will bring your weight down quickly. Once you have lost the weight you need to lose, you can begin to add a little more fat if you choose. But women do not need to go above 50 grams of fat per day to maintain their weight, or men 60. If you are very active and need extra calories, it's far healthier to get them from carbohydrate foods (fruit, vegetables and grains) rather than from fat.

One of the nicest things about using the fat-gram approach to managing your weight is that once you learn where the fat is in your foods and find alternatives for high-fat foods that you can live with, there is no further need to count anything in your effort to maintain desirable weight – neither calories nor fat grams. Just keep on eating the low-fat diet that you design over these next few weeks, and there is no longer any need to keep track of what you are eating.

THE FOURTEEN-DAY MENU PLAN

Begin by making a note of your fat intake using the Fat and Carbohydrate Counter in Appendix C. Use the Fourteen-Day Eating Record at the end of this chapter to monitor your intake over the next two weeks.

The fourteen sample daily menus below usually contain, on the average, about 25 grams of fat, between 210 and 250 grams of carbohydrate, and between 1300 and

1400 calories. If you use these menus, check with Appendix C for the precise nutritional values to enter on the eating chart.

I have intentionally held the fat content of my daily menus down to around 25 grams, to leave room for up to a dessertspoon of added fat each day, which you can use as a spread or in food preparation without exceeding the upper boundaries of the daily fat-gram goals that I have recommended. Add this fat with caution, however, since some people cannot lose weight very efficiently with this much added fat in their diets.

These menus are appropriate to women just as they stand and, together with forty-five to sixty minutes of daily activity, will lead to an average weight loss of between ½ and 1 pound (225–450 g) per week. Men may increase the quantities suggested for main dishes at each meal by 50 per cent (but do not increase the size of desserts and snacks).

Please resist trying to lose weight more quickly. If you have ever used a quick weight-loss programme you must certainly be aware of the difficulty you faced afterward in trying to maintain your weight loss. Your goal in this programme is not simply to 'go on a diet' and then go off it once you have lost weight. That's a recipe for failure. Your task is to find low-fat alternatives for high-fat foods that you can live with permanently, choosing them between 80 and 90 per cent of the time for all your meals and snacks. You don't have to deny yourself completely – just reserve high-fat foods for special occasions, perhaps once or twice a week.

My menus are based on easily obtained foods that will provide you with a nutritious low-fat diet. You can and should, however, substitute foods according to seasonal availability or your own taste preferences.

Take alternatives from the same food group (that is, one meat for another, one fruit for another) and choose foods that have about the same fat content as my examples.[1] In this way the nutritional value of your own daily menus will approximate my examples. Use the Fat and Carbohydrate Counter in Appendix C to keep track.

If you wish to improvise your own daily menus, use the Food Pyramid shown here, and include the recommended number of servings of foods from the various food groups. By eating a variety of foods from within each group you will assure yourself of obtaining all the vitamins and minerals that your body needs. If you keep within the recommended fat-gram goal each day, your own menus will result in carbohydrate and calorie contents that are similar to my menus without your having to make any special effort. Fat is the key. Unless, for one reason or another (such as a food sensitivity), you eliminate from your diet one of the food groups represented in the Food Pyramid, the other nutrients fall into place when you cut the fat without your paying them any special attention.

[1] If you wish to reduce or eliminate animal products, substitute foods such as legumes and grains that will give you equivalent protein from plant sources.

Food Pyramid A/W

Dishes in boldface type in the menus refer to recipes in Chapter 6, where you will find a number of low-fat ways to prepare most of the best-liked foods in the Western diet: beef, poultry, fish, pasta, casseroles, stir-fries and legumes.

MENUS

WEEK 1

Day 1

BREAKFAST
1 ounce/28 g bran flakes, 4 fl oz/110 ml semi-skimmed milk, coffee or tea, 2 tablespoons whole milk

MID-MORNING SNACK
1 fresh peach

LUNCH
Turkey sandwich (2 ounces/56 g breast meat, 2 slices whole-grain bread, chutney or ketchup, 3 tablespoons bean sprouts), 1 ounce/28 g pretzels, 8 fl oz/225 ml skimmed milk

MID-AFTERNOON SNACK
1 orange

DINNER
Pasta (3 ounces/80 g dry weight, cooked) with **Real Italian Tomato Sauce**, 12 fl oz/330 ml measure dinner salad,[1] 1 dessertspoon low-fat dressing, 1 slice Italian or French bread, 1 **Chocolate-Chip Cookie**

---

[1] Based on 8 fl oz/225 ml measure of lettuce and 3 tablespoons each of grated carrots and shredded cabbage, plus a slice of tomato. Feel free to substitute the same total quantity of your own favourite fresh vegetables. The nutritional value will remain similar.

EVENING SNACK
3 Dark Rye Ryvita

Day 2

BREAKFAST
Honey Bran Muffin, 1 apple, coffee or tea, 2 table-spoons whole milk

MID-MORNING SNACK
6 ounces/175 g fresh strawberries

LUNCH
2 ounces/56 g tinned salmon, 1 pitta bread, 3 small carrots and two stalks celery cut into sticks, plus 4 sliced radishes, 8 fl oz/225 ml skimmed milk

MID-AFTERNOON SNACK
3 ounces/80 g seedless grapes

DINNER
1 serving **Marinated Steak**, 1 medium baked potato, 8 fl oz/225 ml measure green beans and water chestnuts, 12 fl oz/330 ml measure dinner salad, 1 dessertspoon low-fat dressing, 8 fl oz/225 ml measure orange and grapefruit sections

EVENING SNACK
3 rice cakes

Day 3

BREAKFAST
1 ounce/28 g shredded wheat, 3 ounces/80 g fresh

strawberries, 4 fl oz/110 ml semi-skimmed milk, coffee
or tea, 2 tablespoons whole milk

MID-MORNING SNACK
1 banana

LUNCH
Chef salad (12 fl oz/330 ml measure dinner salad, 2
ounces/56 g lean ham, ½ ounce/14 g grated cheese, 3
tablespoons croutons), 1 dessertspoon low-fat dressing, 1 slice whole-grain bread, 8 fl oz/225 ml skimmed
milk

MID-AFTERNOON SNACK
2½-inch/1-cm slices fresh pineapple

DINNER
1 serving **Baked Bass with Lemon-Wine Bouillon**, 2
courgettes baked with 1 scant teaspoon butter, 8 fl
oz/225 ml measure brussels sprouts, 8 fl oz/225 ml
measure fresh fruit salad, no-cal beverage

EVENING SNACK
1 slice fruit bread, toasted, 1 scant teaspoon jam or jelly,
1 small carton low-fat yoghurt.

Day 4

BREAKFAST
1 warm bagel, 1 scant teaspoon jelly or marmalade, 1
banana, coffee or tea, 2 tablespoons whole milk

MID-MORNING SNACK
1 medium apple

LUNCH
Turkey sandwich (2 ounces/56 g sliced turkey breast, 2 slices whole-grain bread, 1 leaf lettuce, 2 slices tomato, 1½ teaspoons mild mustard), 8 fl oz/225 ml measure orange and grapefruit sections, no-cal beverage

MID-AFTERNOON SNACK
3 Dark Rye Ryvita

DINNER
1 small serving **Indian Spiced Beans**, 2 ounces/56 g, dry weight cooked brown rice, 4 fl oz/110 ml measure spinach, 1 **New England Corn Muffin**, 12 fl oz/330 ml measure dinner salad, 1 dessertspoon low-fat dressing, no-cal beverage

EVENING SNACK
3 rice cakes

Day 5

BREAKFAST
1 egg cooked without fat, 1 slice whole-grain toast, 1 teaspoon low-fat spread, 1 scant teaspoon marmalade or jelly, coffee or tea, 2 tablespoons whole milk

MID-MORNING SNACK
½ grapefruit

LUNCH
8 fl oz/225 ml clear soup, ½ sandwich (1 slice whole-wheat bread, 1 ounce/28 g lean ham, 1 leaf lettuce, 1 slice tomato, 1 scant teaspoon mustard), 2 medium carrots cut into sticks, 8 fl oz/225 ml skimmed milk

MID-AFTERNOON SNACK
3 ounces/80 g grapes

DINNER
1 serving **Oven-Fried Chicken**, 1 medium baked potato with 1 scant teaspoon butter, 2 small courgettes, 12 fl oz/330 ml measure dinner salad, 1 dessertspoon low-fat dressing, 1 slice whole-grain bread, no-cal beverage

EVENING SNACK
6 ounces/175 g fresh strawberries

Day 6

BREAKFAST
1 ounce/28 g bran flakes, ½ sliced banana, 4 fl oz/110 ml semi-skimmed milk, coffee or tea, 2 tablespoons whole milk

MID-MORNING SNACK
4 fl oz/110 ml grapefruit juice

LUNCH
8fl oz/225 ml non-cream vegetable soup, 1 **New England Corn Muffin**, 1 peach, no-cal beverage

MID-AFTERNOON SNACK
2 rice cakes

DINNER
3 ounces/80 g lean, well-trimmed pork loin, 1 medium sweet potato, 12 fl oz/330 ml measure tossed salad, 1 dessertspoon low-fat dressing, 1 slice whole-grain bread

EVENING SNACK
1 small carton low-fat yoghurt

Day 7

BREAKFAST
Porridge made with 6 fl oz/180 ml boiling water and 2-3 level tablespoons rolled oats, 1 dessertspoon sultanas or raisins, ¼ teaspoon cinnamon, 1 scant teaspoon light brown sugar, 4 fl oz/110 ml semi-skimmed milk, coffee or tea, 2 tablespoons whole milk

MID-MORNING SNACK
⅛ honeydew melon

LUNCH
Tuna salad (3 ounces/80 g tinned tuna packed in brine, 1½ teaspoons low-fat mayonnaise, 1 scant teaspoon Worcestershire sauce, 1 small stalk celery chopped, 1 spring onion chopped, 3 leaves lettuce, 2 slices tomato), 2 slices whole-grain bread, no-cal beverage

MID-AFTERNOON SNACK
1 small carton low-fat yoghurt

DINNER
1 serving **Japanese Beef Stir-Fry**, 2 ounces/56 g, dry weight brown rice, cooked, 12 fl oz/330 ml measure dinner salad, 1 dessertspoon low-fat dressing, 1 two-inch/5-cm diameter whole-grain roll, 8 fl oz/225 ml measure fresh fruit salad, no-cal beverage

EVENING SNACK
1 ounce bran flakes, 4 fl oz/110 ml semi-skimmed milk

WEEK 2

Day 8

BREAKFAST
Honey Bran Muffin, 4 fl oz/110 ml measure of grape-fruit segments, coffee or tea, 2 tablespoons whole milk

MID-MORNING SNACK
1 nectarine

LUNCH
8 fl oz/225 ml non-cream vegetable soup, 1 ounce/28 g breadsticks, 2 medium carrots and 2 stalks celery cut into sticks, 4 radishes, 1 fresh peach, no-cal beverage

MID-AFTERNOON SNACK
3 Dark Rye Ryvita

DINNER
1 serving **Chicken Divan**, 2 ounces/56 g, dry weight brown rice, cooked, small serving steamed broccoli, 1 two-inch/5-cm-diameter dinner roll, 4 fl oz/110 ml measure stewed fruit with 1 dessertspoon Grape Nuts, 8 fl oz/225 ml skimmed milk

EVENING SNACK
1 banana

Day 9

BREAKFAST
1 ounce Cheerios, ½ sliced banana, 4 fl oz/110 ml semi-skimmed milk, coffee or tea, 2 tablespoons whole milk

MID-MORNING SNACK
2 plums

LUNCH
Salmon salad (2 ounces/56 g tinned salmon, 1½ tea-spoons low-fat mayonnaise, 1 scant teaspoon Worcestershire sauce, 1 small stalk celery chopped, 1 spring onion chopped, 3 leaves lettuce, 2 slices tomato, 3 tablespoons bean sprouts), 1 bagel, 8 fl oz/225 ml skimmed milk

MID-AFTERNOON SNACK
1 small carton low-fat yoghurt

DINNER
1 serving **Lemon-Pepper Beef**, 3 ounces/80 g pasta, dry weight, 1 serving brussels sprouts, 1 slice whole-grain bread, 12 fl oz/330 ml measure dinner salad, 1 dessert-spoon low-fat dressing, no-cal beverage

EVENING SNACK
8 fl oz/225 ml measure orange and grapefruit sections

Day 10

BREAKFAST
1 egg, poached or boiled, 2 slices whole-grain bread, 1½ teaspoons low-fat spread, coffee or tea, 2 tablespoons whole milk

MID-MORNING SNACK
1 tangerine

LUNCH
Chef salad (12 fl oz/330 ml measure dinner salad, 2

141

ounces/56 g white-meat turkey, ½ ounce/14 g grated cheese, 3 tablespoons croutons), 1 dessertspoon low-fat dressing, 1 slice whole-grain bread, 8 fl oz/225 ml skimmed milk

MID-AFTERNOON SNACK
1 small carton low-fat yoghurt

DINNER
1 serving **Fish Florentine**, 1 small serving steamed carrots, 2 ounces/56 g, dry weight wild rice, cooked, 1 two-inch/5-cm-diameter whole-grain roll, no-cal beverage

EVENING SNACK
3 ounces/80 g fresh strawberries

Day 11

BREAKFAST
Porridge made with 6 fl oz/180 ml boiling water and 2–3 level tablespoons rolled oats, 1 dessertspoon sultanas or raisins, ¼ teaspoon cinnamon, 1 scant teaspoon light brown sugar, 4 fl oz/125 ml semi-skimmed milk, coffee or tea, 2 tablespoons whole milk

MID-MORNING SNACK
1 banana

LUNCH
Tuna-stuffed tomato (3 ounces/80 g tinned brine-packed tuna, 1½ teaspoons low-fat mayonnaise, 1 scant teaspoon Worcestershire sauce, 1 small stalk celery chopped, 1 large hollowed-out tomato), 1 pitta bread, 8 fl oz/225 ml skimmed milk

MID-AFTERNOON SNACK
1 orange

DINNER
1 serving **Turkey Chop Suey**, 1 two-inch/5-cm-diameter whole-grain roll, 12 fl oz/330 ml measure dinner salad, 1 dessertspoon low-fat dressing, no-cal beverage

EVENING SNACK
1 small carton plain very low fat yoghurt, 3 ounces/80 g raspberries or 1 kiwi fruit, sliced

Day 12

BREAKFAST
2 slices fruit bread, toasted, 1 scant teaspoon jelly or marmalade, 1½ teaspoons low-fat spread, coffee or tea, 2 tablespoons whole milk

MID-MORNING SNACK
½ grapefruit

LUNCH
Spinach salad (3 ounces/80 g fresh spinach leaves, chopped, 3 tablespoons sliced mushrooms, 2 slices red onion, ½ hard-boiled egg, ½ ounce/14 g grated low-fat white cheese), 1 dessertspoon low-fat dressing, 1 slice whole-grain toast, no-cal beverage

MID-AFTERNOON SNACK
1 small carton low-fat yoghurt

DINNER
1 serving **Vegetarian Chilli Texas Style**, 2 ounces/56 g,
dry weight, brown rice, cooked, 1 serving steamed
asparagus, 1 slice whole-wheat bread, no-cal beverage

EVENING SNACK
8 fl oz/225 ml measure orange and grapefruit sections

Day 13

BREAKFAST
1 ounce/28 g bran flakes, 4 fl oz/110 ml semi-skimmed
milk, coffee or tea, 2 tablespoons whole milk

MID-MORNING SNACK
1/8 honeydew melon

LUNCH
Medium baked potato (topped with 3 ounces/80 g low-
fat cottage cheese, 1 spring onion, diced, 3 tablespoons
diced sweet green peppers, pepper seasoning), 2 small
to medium carrots, cut in sticks, no-cal beverage

MID-AFTERNOON SNACK
1 orange

DINNER
1 serving **Chicken Cacciatore**, 1 serving green beans, 12
fl oz/330 ml measure dinner salad, 1 dessertspoon low-
fat dressing, 4 fl oz/110 ml measure stewed fruit with
1 dessertspoon Grape Nuts, 8 fl oz/225 ml skimmed
milk

EVENING SNACK
1 apple

Day 14

BREAKFAST
Porridge made with 6 fl oz/180 ml boiling water and
2–3 tablespoons rolled oats, 1 dessertspoon sultanas or
raisins, ¼ teaspoon cinnamon, 1 scant teaspoon light
brown sugar, 4 fl oz/110 ml semi-skimmed milk, coffee
or tea, 2 tablespoons whole milk.

MID-MORNING SNACK
1 banana

LUNCH
8 fl oz/225 ml non-cream vegetable soup, 1 **New
England Corn Muffin**, no-cal beverage

MID-AFTERNOON SNACK
1 small carton low-fat yoghurt

DINNER
1 serving **Spinach Lasagna**, 1 two-inch/15-cm-
diameter whole-grain roll, 12 fl oz/330 ml measure of
dinner salad, 1 dessertspoon low-fat dressing, no-cal
beverage

EVENING SNACK
8 fl oz/125 ml measure of orange and grapefruit
sections

SUPPOSING THE DIET AND ACTIVITY PROGRAMME DOES NOT SEEM TO BE WORKING FOR YOU?

If the simple approach that I have just outlined does not seem to be working, you must first make sure you are really doing what I have asked you to do!

Research shows that almost everyone, including trained dieticians, underestimates their fat intake by 10 to 20 grams a day. Fat is well hidden in foods, especially in animal and dairy products, desserts and snacks. Even identical foods labelled low-fat and lean, but produced by different manufacturers, can vary by several grams of fat in portions of identical size. Ask yourself:

Am I certain about the fat content of the processed foods and animal and dairy products that I am eating?

Am I keeping track of everything I eat?

Have I recorded the portions accurately?

When I use any added fat, do I know what a *level* or *scant* teaspoon or dessertspoon of fat, oil or salad dressing looks like, so that I can be certain I am not underestimating added fat?

When you are certain that your fat intake is being accurately represented in your records, and you still have difficulty managing your weight, then it's time to take a look at carbohydrates.

From our previous discussion you already know that, in people who are weight-stable, the body converts almost no carbohydrate to fat. Small daily variations in carbohydrate consumption lead only to changes in glucose and water stores. Together with variations in your sodium intake, variation in carbohydrate consumption is one of the main dietary factors that leads to daily weight fluctuations that can amount to several pounds. With fat, however, 97 per cent of excess fat calories at any given meal will go directly to your fat cells.

However, you cannot overdo carbohydrates continually without forcing your body to convert more and more of the carbohydrate calories to fat. For example, if you continually outeat your energy needs for a week, your body will gradually work up from about 4 per cent conversion of excess carbohydrate to fat to about 75 per cent.

Some people have actually made the mistake of believing that once they have their fat content down to the level I recommend, they can eat anything they want so long as it contains little or no fat. So (and these are actual reports in my files) they added to their daily diets two extra loaves of bread, or two family-size bags of pretzels, or six packages of jelly beans. This amounts to between 200 and 400 extra grams of carbohydrate and 1000 to 2000 extra calories. You can't do this on a daily basis and expect to lose weight!

If bringing your fat intake into the range I have set for you does not seem to be working, begin by setting the following carbohydrate limit as your starting point:

Women   250 grams of carbohydrate per day
Men   300 grams of carbohydrate per day

Keep track of your daily intake of carbohydrate together with fat in grams. Use the Fat and Carbohydrate Counter in Appendix C.

Women should keep their daily fat consumption to

20–25 grams, and men 30–35 grams. If the carbohydrate intake I've just recommended does not lead to weight loss, begin to decrease carbohydrates. Women may go as low as 200 grams and men to 250 grams per day. If you eat a wide variety of foods from each of the food groups (use the Food Pyramid shown earlier in this chapter), you will still be consuming a nutritious diet.

If you are certain your eating record is accurate, and my recommendations still do not work in spite of your meeting a *daily* activity goal of *at least* forty-five minutes of walking (or its equivalent), I suggest that you consult either your doctor or a qualified dietician for help. Something is wrong that requires personal, professional supervision.

Fourteen-day
Eating
Record Charts

FOURTEEN-DAY EATING RECORD

Column Headings: FAT = FAT; CARB = CARBOHYDRATE; CAL = CALORIES.
List the foods you eat at all meals and for snacks. Look up the fat and carbohydrate grams, and the calories, in the Fat and Carbohydrate Counter in Appendix C. Keep this record for the next fourteen days. Make additional copies to continue

	DAY 1			DAY 2			DAY 3		
DATE BEGUN	F A T	C A R B	C A L	F A T	C A R B	C A L	F A T	C A R B	C A L
BREAKFAST									
SNACK									
LUNCH									
SNACK									
DINNER									
SNACK									
TOTAL									

for more than fourteen days. Continue to keep a record for at least three weeks if you have just stopped smoking.

Fat-gram targets: Women   20–40 grams per day
                           Men   30–60 grams

DAY 4			DAY 5			DAY 6			DAY 7		
FAT	CARB	CAL	FAT	CARB	CAL	FAT	CARB	CAL	FAT	CARB	CAL

DATE BEGUN	DAY 8			DAY 9			DAY 10		
	F A T	C A R B	C A L	F A T	C A R B	C A L	F A T	C A R B	C A L
BREAKFAST									
SNACK									
LUNCH									
SNACK									
DINNER									
SNACK									
TOTAL									

DAY 11			DAY 12			DAY 13			DAY 14		
F A T	C A R B	C A L	F A T	C A R B	C A L	F A T	C A R B	C A L	F A T	C A R B	C A L

6

Recipes

The recipes that follow illustrate some basic ways to prepare a number of favourite dishes. Pay attention to the basic ingredients, especially the amount of added fat, which is always kept to a minimum consistent with good taste. Adapt your own favourite recipes for fish, poultry, meat, casseroles and so on, using the suggestions for food preparation for the dinner meal in Table 3 of Chapter 3, and your recipes will be similar to mine in their fat, carbohydrate and calorie values.

BAKED BASS WITH LEMON-WINE BOUILLON

4 fillets bass, haddock OR other thick white fish, about
    1 pound/450 k raw
½ teaspoon dried chives
¼ teaspoon dried chervil OR dried parsley
¼ teaspoon dried tarragon
1 dessertspoon lemon juice (fresh is best!)
4 fl oz/110 ml dry white wine
3 tablespoons bread crumbs
1 dessertspoon butter OR margarine

1. Place the fillets in a shallow baking dish. Sprinkle
   with seasonings and lemon juice. Pour the wine over
   the fish.
2. Bake at 400°F/Gas 6/200°C for 15 minutes. Then
   sprinkle the bread crumbs on top, and dot with
   butter. Bake 15 minutes more, or until fish flakes
   easily with a fork.

4 Servings of 3½ ounces/100 g each (cooked weight)

Per serving: **7 g fat**, 10 g carbohydrate, 209 calories, 75
mg cholesterol, 1 g dietary fibre, 208 mg sodium

FISH FLORENTINE

This Italian style of cooking (with spinach) works as
well with veal and chicken.

1 pound/450 g fish fillets (plaice or sole)
1 package (10 ounces/300 g) frozen chopped spinach, thawed
    and drained
10 whole-wheat crackers, crushed

1½ tablespoons wheat germ
2 tablespoons Parmesan cheese

1. Arrange the fillets in the bottom of a shallow baking dish.
2. Cover the fish with the well-drained spinach.
3. Combine the cracker crumbs, wheat germ and cheese, and pour over the fish and spinach.
4. Bake, uncovered, at 400°F/Gas 6/200°C for 15 to 20 minutes.

4 *Servings of 3 ounces/100 g each (cooked weight), plus spinach*

Per serving: **4 g fat**, 9 g carbohydrate, 181 calories, 62 mg cholesterol, 2 g dietary fibre, 296 mg sodium

CHICKEN DIVAN

6 chicken breasts, boned and skinned, 5 ounces/145 g each
12 fl oz/330 ml chicken stock
3 tablespoons whole-wheat flour
6 fl oz/175 ml skimmed milk
4 tablespoons low-fat dried milk
4 tablespoons white wine
large pinch pepper
1½ pounds/700 g fresh broccoli OR 2 packages (10 ounces/300 g each) frozen broccoli spears
3 ounces/80 g Parmesan cheese, grated
1 tablespoon fresh parsley, chopped

1. Wrap the chicken breasts in aluminium foil and bake at 350°F/Gas 4/180°C for 30 minutes.
2. Meanwhile, bring the chicken stock to a boil.

3. In another pan over low heat, combine 4 tablespoons of the boiling stock and the flour. Cook and stir until smooth. Gradually add the rest of the stock, stirring until thickened. Remove from heat.
4. Combine the skimmed and dried milk, and add to the stock, along with the wine and pepper.
5. If using raw broccoli blanch the spears for 3 minutes in boiling water. Place the broccoli in a shallow baking dish. Top with half the sauce. Arrange the cooked chicken breasts on top of the broccoli. Combine half the cheese with the rest of the sauce, and pour over the chicken. Sprinkle with parsley and the remaining cheese, and bake at 350°F/Gas 4/180°C for 20 minutes.

6 Servings of 1 breast, plus vegetables

Per serving: **6 g fat**, 12 g carbohydrate, 260 calories, 81 mg cholesterol, 3 g dietary fibre, 292 mg sodium

CHICKEN CACCIATORE

1 small onion, chopped
1 clove garlic, minced (or ⅓ teaspoon garlic powder)
3 tablespoons water
1 14½-ounce/400-g tin whole tomatoes, chopped
1 6-ounce/175-g tin tomato paste
1 scant teaspoon oregano
Salt and fresh-ground black pepper to taste
4 chicken breasts, skinless and boneless
8 ounces/225 g rice OR 12 ounces/350 g spaghetti, dry weight, cooked and hot

1. In a large pan over medium heat, cook onion and

garlic with water, covered, for 5 minutes or until onion is tender.

2. Stir in the tomatoes, tomato paste and seasonings. Reduce heat, cover and simmer for 10–15 minutes.
3. Add the chicken and cook, covered, for 30 minutes. Uncover and cook another 15 minutes.
4. Serve over spaghetti or rice.

4 Servings

Per serving with 1 cup spaghetti: **5 g fat**, 54 g carbohydrate, 402 calories, 73 mg cholesterol, 6 g dietary fibre, 394 mg sodium

OVEN-FRIED CHICKEN

1 dessertspoon vegetable oil
1 teaspoon lemon juice
3 pounds/1350 g chicken pieces, skinned
About 3 tablespoons skimmed or semi-skimmed milk OR *buttermilk.*
2 ounces/56 g flour, plain, wholemeal or a combination
1½ teaspoons paprika
¼ teaspoon salt
¼ teaspoon black pepper
¼ teaspoon onion powder
¼ teaspoon garlic powder
⅛ teaspoon cayenne pepper
¼ teaspoon marjoram
¼ teaspoon oregano

1. Combine the oil and lemon juice, and brush each piece of skinned chicken with the mixture.
2. Place the milk in a shallow bowl, and set aside.

Combine the flour(s) and seasonings in another bowl, mixing well.

3. Dip the chicken into the milk, coating all sides. Then coat with flour mixture.

4. Place the chicken 'skin' side down in a foil-covered baking dish. Cover loosely with foil, and bake at 350°F/Gas 4/180°C for 30 minutes. Turn the chicken pieces over, and bake 30 minutes more, or until cooked through.

6 Servings of 3½ ounces/100 g each (cooked weight)

Per serving: **7 g fat**, 9 g carbohydrate, 233 calories, 89 mg cholesterol, 1 g dietary fibre, 180 mg sodium

TURKEY CHOP SUEY

1 pound/450 g minced turkey
1 tin (16 ounces/450 g) bean sprouts, drained OR *12 ounces/350 g fresh bean sprouts*
3 stalks celery, chopped
1 onion, chopped
1 tin (8 ounces/225 g) water chestnuts, drained and sliced
1 tin (5 ounces/145 g) sliced mushrooms, drained
¼ teaspoon ground ginger
1 tin (10½ ounces/315 g) condensed beef or chicken consommé
2 dessertspoons soy sauce
2 dessertspoons cornflour (or 1 ounce/28 g flour)
12 ounces/350 g brown rice, cooked

1. In a large pan, brown the turkey. Drain off any fat.
2. Add the vegetables, ginger and all but 4 tablespoons of the consommé. Bring to a boil over medium-high heat. Reduce heat, cover, and simmer for 20 minutes.

3. Combine the reserved broth with the soy sauce and cornflour. Add to the meat and vegetable mixture, stirring until thickened and bubbly. Serve over the rice.

6 Servings

Per serving: **7 g fat**, 34 g carbohydrate, 309 calories, 64 mg cholesterol, 4 g dietary fibre, 693 mg sodium

LEMON-PEPPER BEEF

1 pound/450 g lean topside or steak, well trimmed
4 tablespoons dry red wine
1½ to 2 tablespoons lemon juice
⅓ teaspoon salt
1 bay leaf
2 yellow or red sweet peppers, cut in eighths
Fresh-ground black pepper to taste

1. Combine all ingredients in a large covered plastic, china or glass bowl and marinate overnight, or at least 6 hours, in the refrigerator. Turn beef and peppers occasionally.
2. Place beef on grill pan at medium heat and grill for about 8 minutes. Turn, and add the pepper pieces to the pan. After 6 minutes or so, turn the peppers over, then grill about 4 minutes more for medium-well-done beef. Slice the beef thinly across the grain, and serve with the peppers.

4 Servings of 3 ounces each (cooked weight)

Per serving: **4 g fat**, 4 g carbohydrate, 177 calories, 71 mg cholesterol, 1 g dietary fibre, 320 mg sodium

MARINATED STEAK

1 pound/450 g lean grilling steak in one piece
3 spring onions, chopped
2 cloves garlic
2 dessertspoons soy sauce
1 tablespoon red wine
1 tablespoon water
1 teaspoon olive oil

Combine all ingredients in a large covered plastic, glass or china bowl and marinate for at least 4 hours (preferably overnight) in the refrigerator. Use marinade for basting while grilling or baking.

Variation: Mince a 1-inch/12-cm piece of fresh ginger (peeled) and add to the marinade for an oriental flavour.

4 Servings of 3 ounces/800 g each (cooked weight)

Per serving: **10 g fat**, 1 g carbohydrate, 194 calories, 57 mg cholesterol, 0 dietary fibre, 477 mg sodium

JAPANESE BEEF STIR-FRY

4 beef fillet steaks (about 4 ounces/110 g each)
1 dessertspoon peanut oil
12 ounces/350 g mange-tout peas, fresh or frozen and thawed
¼ head red cabbage, thinly sliced
¼ inch/½ cm fresh ginger, minced, OR ground ginger to taste
1 dessertspoon saké or dry sherry (optional)
Dash tamari sauce OR soy sauce

1. Heat a wok or heavy pan over medium-high heat for

162

several minutes. Meanwhile, trim the beef of all visible fat and slice into thin slices.

2. Add the oil to the pan, then the beef. Cook, stirring constantly, until browned.
3. Lower the heat to medium, remove the meat from the pan, and set aside.
4. Add the peas, cabbage and ginger to the wok, and cook for 5 minutes, stirring constantly.
5. Return the meat to the wok, and stir in the saké and the soy sauce. Cover, and let simmer for a few more minutes, until the vegetables are just tender and the meat is cooked the way you like it.

4 Servings of 3 ounces/80 g each (cooked weight), plus vegetables

Per serving: **12 g fat**, 9 g carbohydrate, 260 calories, 71 mg cholesterol, 3 g dietary fibre, 81 mg sodium

SPINACH LASAGNA

8 ounces/225 g lasagna, preferably whole-wheat
1 medium onion, chopped
2 cloves garlic, minced
1 dessertspoon olive oil
Water as needed
1 pound/450 g low-fat cottage cheese
3 tablespoons grated Parmesan
1½ pounds/675 g fresh spinach, cooked, chopped and well drained OR *1 10-ounce/300g package frozen chopped spinach, thawed and drained*
2 egg whites, beaten
¼ teaspoon fresh-ground black pepper
2 to 3 tablespoons fresh parsley, chopped

3 9-ounce/265-g jars tomato or other meatless spaghetti sauce
6 ounces/175 g (low-fat if possible) mozzarella, grated

1. Cook the lasagna according to package directions.
2. While it is cooking, sauté the onion and garlic in the olive oil, adding a tablespoon or two of water as needed to keep from sticking.
3. Combine the cottage cheese, Parmesan, spinach, egg whites, black pepper, parsley and sautéed onion and garlic, mixing well.
4. Lightly oil a warmed 9 x 13 x 2-inch casserole dish (23 x 30 x 5-cm). Spread ¼ of the tomato or spaghetti sauce over the bottom and then arrange a layer of lasagne, top with ⅓ of the cheese-spinach mixture, sprinkle with ⅓ of the mozzarella, and top with tomato sauce. Repeat layers twice more, ending with sauce.
5. Cover the dish with foil, crimping edges tightly. Bake at 350°F/Gas 4/180°C for 40 minutes; remove foil and bake 10–15 minutes more.

12 Servings

Per serving (using partly skimmed mozzarella): **5 g fat**, 28 g carbohydrate, 213 calories, 12 mg cholesterol, 4 g dietary fibre, 903 mg sodium

REAL ITALIAN TOMATO SAUCE

1 dessertspoon olive oil
1 medium onion, cut in chunks
8 oz/225 g fresh mushrooms, sliced or quartered
1–2 tablespoons dried basil (even more if you use fresh!)
2 large cloves garlic, crushed or minced

1 large bay leaf
28 oz/800 g tin tomatoes
11 oz/325 g tin tomato purée
6 oz/175 g tin tomato paste
salt and fresh-ground black pepper to taste

1. Heat a large saucepan over medium heat. Put in the oil, onion, mushrooms, basil and garlic. Cover, and reduce the heat to medium low. Stir frequently – you may need to add a tablespoon or two of water to keep it from sticking.
2. When the onions are translucent, add the remaining ingredients, except the salt and pepper. Bring to a boil on high heat, then reduce to simmer and let cook for an hour or so, stirring occasionally and breaking up the whole tomatoes.
3. Add salt and pepper to taste.

6 Servings

Per serving: **2 g fat**, 23 g carbohydrate, 107 calories, 0 cholesterol, 6 g dietary fibre, 650 mg sodium

INDIAN SPICED BEANS

12 ounces/350 g dried red or kidney beans
1½ pints/850 ml stock
1 medium onion, sliced
1 medium tomato, chopped
1 clove garlic, chopped
2 dried red chillies
1 bay leaf
¼ teaspoon fresh-ground black pepper
¼ teaspoon ground cloves

Wash beans and remove any stones. Place all ingredients in a large saucepan. Bring to a boil and let boil for 10 minutes, then reduce heat. Cover and cook for 4 hours on low heat.

6 Servings, each measuring 6 fl oz/330 ml.

Per serving: **2 g fat**, 42 g carbohydrate, 248 calories, 0 cholesterol, 14 g dietary fibre, 230 mg sodium

VEGETARIAN CHILLI TEXAS STYLE

2 medium-size onions, chopped
4 cloves garlic, minced
16 fl oz/450 ml vegetable stock
1 15-ounce/425-g tin whole tomatoes, cut up, with juice
1 6-ounce/175-g tin tomato paste
2 tablespoons chilli powder
1 teaspoon vinegar (cider or red wine)
1 scant teaspoon ground cumin
½ teaspoon ground coriander
½ teaspoon oregano
¼ teaspoon fresh-ground black pepper
3 whole dried red peppers (hot)
2 16-ounce/450-g cans red or kidney beans, drained

1. In a large saucepan, simmer the onions and garlic in 3 tablespoons of the stock until translucent.
2. Add all remaining ingredients except the beans and simmer for 45 minutes.
3. Add beans and simmer for another 15 minutes.

8 Servings each measuring 8 fl oz/225 ml

Per serving: **1 g fat**, 34 g carbohydrate, 179 calories, 0 cholesterol, 12 g dietary fibre, 622 mg sodium

HONEY BRAN MUFFINS

6 ounces/175 g All Bran cereal
4 tablespoons honey
10 fl oz/275 ml skimmed milk
1 egg
4 ounces/110 g plain flour
1 teaspoon baking powder
$^1/_3$ teaspoon salt

1. Combine the cereal, honey and milk, and let stand for
   2 minutes. Add the egg, beating well.
2. Stir together the flour, baking powder and salt; add
   to the cereal mixture, stirring *only until combined*.
   Portion the batter evenly into lightly greased 2½-inch
   muffin cups.
3. Bake at 400°F/Gas 6/200°C for 25 minutes or until a
   toothpick inserted in the centre of a muffin comes out
   clean. Let stand about 5 minutes before removing
   from the pan. Serve immediately.

12 Muffins

Per muffin: **1 g fat**, 28 g carbohydrate, 117 calories, 16
mg cholesterol, 5 g dietary fibre, 337 mg sodium

NEW ENGLAND CORN MUFFINS

7 tablespoons honey
2 eggs plus 3 egg whites
14 fl oz/400 ml skimmed milk
3 tablespoons vegetable oil
2 ounces/56 g sugar
2 dessertspoons baking powder
14 ounces/400 g plain flour

5 ounces/145 g cornmeal or maizemeal
¼ teaspoon salt

1. In a large bowl, whisk together the honey, eggs and egg whites, milk and oil.
2. Add the dry ingredients and mix with an electric mixer at medium-high speed for 2 minutes.
3. Lightly oil two warmed muffin tins or line with baking cups. Fill each cup ¾ full. Bake at 400°F/Gas 6/200°C for about 15 minutes, or until tops are golden brown.

24 Muffins

Per muffin: **3 g fat**, 25 g carbohydrate, 145 calories, 23 mg cholesterol, 1 g dietary fibre, 104 mg sodium

CHOCOLATE-CHIP COOKIES

4 ounces/110 g butter, softened
3½ ounces/95 g soft brown sugar
4 ounces/110 g granulated sugar
1 scant teaspoon vanilla essence
1 teaspoon water
2 eggs
5 ounces/145 g wholemeal flour
4 ounces/110 g plain flour
1 teaspoon baking powder
1 scant teaspoon salt
6 ounces/175 g dark chocolate chips
4 ounces/110 g chopped nuts

1. Preheat the oven to 375°F/Gas 5/190°C.
2. In a large bowl, combine the butter, sugars, vanilla essence and water. Beat in the egg.

3. In another bowl, combine the flours, baking powder and salt. Gradually add this to the wet ingredients, blending well. Stir in the chocolate chips and the nuts.
4. Drop by rounded teaspoonsful onto Teflon baking sheets. Bake until golden brown, about 8 to 10 minutes.

Variation: Add a couple of teaspoons of grated orange rind to the batter before baking, for Orange Chocolate-Chip Cookies.

3 dozen cookies, about 2 inches/5 cm in diameter

Per cookie: **5 g fat**, 13 g carbohydrate, 99 calories, about 12 mg cholesterol, 1 g dietary fibre, 114 mg sodium

Appendix A

STRENGTH-TRAINING ROUTINE

Strength training builds muscles. Because muscle cells are more active around the clock than fat cells, building muscles increases your resting metabolic rate. This will help combat the metabolic slowdown that occurs when you stop smoking. In addition, strength-training exercises burn a relatively high percentage of glucose in your fuel mixture, compared with fat. This can help burn off any excess carbohydrate that you may consume in an attempt to alleviate some of the symptoms that occur when you stop smoking.

It's generally best for women just starting a strength-training programme to use 3-pound (1.4-kilo) weights and for men to use 5-pound or 3-kilo (6.6 pound) weights. You can use books instead of weights. You can increase the weights by a few pounds as your strength increases. However, to avoid injury, it is generally better to increase the repetitions of the training movements rather than attempt to use very heavy weights.

The following set of exercises focuses on your upper body, legs and stomach. You will find additional exercises in the booklet that comes with a set of weights. You can often get supervision in the development of a strength-training programme at your local health club or sports centre.

Be sure to check with your doctor before beginning any new fitness programme.

UPPER BODY SERIES

1. *Two for the shoulders.* Hold arms at your sides with palms facing the rear. Keeping arms straight, raise weights forward to shoulder height and return to down position, slowly and with control. Breathe normally at all times. Work up to 10 repetitions, then rest for at least one deep breath. Then turn the weights so that your palms face your body, and raise your arms outward to the sides, up to shoulder level. Work up to 10 repetitions.

2. *Biceps curl.* Stand straight with arms at sides, palms facing forward. Curl forearms up to shoulder 10 times at a moderate pace.

3. *Triceps.* Keeping elbows next to your body, bend forward at about a 60-degree angle from the hips, and curl forearms, bringing weights up to your shoulders. Then, keeping elbows next to your body, straighten

your arms out behind you. Repeat until you feel some strain and stop. This will build the muscle on the back of your arms, and help reduce the likelihood of loose skin on your upper arms if you have been losing weight.

4. *Forward, up and out.* Standing upright, start with arms at your sides, palms facing body. Curling at the elbows, bring weights forward and up almost to the shoulders. Continuing in one uninterrupted motion, spread arms out to your sides, shoulder level, palms facing forward. Keep your arms slightly bent to avoid excessive strain. Return along the same path as you began and repeat up to 10 times.

LEG SERIES

5. *Heel lifts.* With weights at your side, go up and down slowly on your toes several times, resting about a second at the top each time.

6. *Half squats.* (If you are more than a few pounds overweight, don't use any extra weight for this exercise.) With arms at sides, feet at shoulder width, toes facing slightly out, squat down one-third to half the way to the floor. Do not go beyond the point where your thighs are parallel to the floor, and keep your knees over your feet when squatting.

STOMACH SERIES

7. *Bent-knee sit-up.* Lie on your back with knees bent and feet close to your buttocks. Curl your head and shoulders about halfway up to your knees to begin

with. (As you get stronger, try to get closer to your knees.) Roll back down. Arms can be held out in front of you to start with, and then, as you get stronger, they can be folded across your chest. Ultimately, hands are held behind your head.

8. *Reverse sit-up.* Lying flat on the floor with arms at your sides, bring your heels back to your buttocks, and then lift knees to your chest, raising hips off the floor. Return to starting position and repeat several times. Breathe normally.

Finally, one of the very best strengthening exercises of all is the push-up, but it should not be undertaken until your stomach muscles are reasonably strong and until you can do a push-up resting on your knees rather than your toes. You can practise some easier versions of the push-up by pushing off against a wall until you get stronger.

Appendix B

RELAXATION TRAINING AND MEDITATION

DEEP MUSCULAR RELAXATION

You can achieve both mental and physical relaxation with a technique called 'deep muscular relaxation'. It works because, with mentally focused training, tensed muscles can become more relaxed than they were prior to the tension. When deep muscular relaxation training is combined with the specific 'breath of relaxation' that I will show you as you practise the complete technique, you can achieve almost instantaneous physical and mental relief. The technique has proved to be of great value to people who face great tension and who need to be able to relax instantly in order to achieve maximum performance, for example athletes before they start their brief spurt of activity.

Training begins by tensing and relaxing various sets of muscles throughout your body. This will enable you to experience the relaxed state you are aiming for. After a few days of practise, you will no longer need to tense your muscles before relaxing them. You will simply use the 'breath of relaxation' and let loose in any region of your body where you feel tension. At the same time you clear your mind for a few moments, and then make a new beginning at whatever you were doing.

You will need to set aside about twenty minutes on each of the next few days for practice. You should be sitting in a comfortable chair (with or without arms) in a quiet place where you will not be disturbed. If your chair has no arms, rest your hands in your lap, except when the exercise calls for hand movements.

When you tense your muscles during training, go only to about three-quarters of their maximum tension. More is not needed. Do each exercise twice, relax for 5 or 10 seconds in between, then proceed to the next.

You can do these exercises with your eyes open or closed, but you will probably be more focused and relaxed afterwards if you do them with your eyes closed. Remember to breathe normally throughout except in the special breathing exercise.

THE DEEP MUSCULAR RELAXATION TRAINING ROUTINE

1. Make a fist with your right hand. Hold it for 5 seconds, focusing on the tension in the muscles in your hand and up your arm. Relax, and note the difference between the tension and the relaxation.

2. Make fists with both hands. Hold for 5 seconds, noting feelings in the muscles involved. Relax.

Always remember to focus on the difference in the feelings in your muscles as you do the tension part of the exercise, and contrast that with the feelings as you let go and relax. It helps to think 'Let go' as you relax.

3. Make fists with both hands and slowly raise your forearms up to your shoulders, imagining that you are lifting fairly heavy weights. Hold for 5 seconds, then relax ('let go') and return your arms to the resting position.

The next seven exercises are for the head, neck and shoulders, which are focal points for tension in most people.

4. Raise your eyebrows as far as you can. Hold for 5 seconds. Relax.

5. Crease your forehead (bringing your eyebrows together). Hold for 5 seconds. Relax.

6. Press your lips together. Hold for 5 seconds. Relax.

7. Scrunch up your whole face (make a 'funny face'; it doesn't matter exactly how, just so long as you feel some tension in several muscle areas of your face). Hold for 5 seconds. Relax.

8. Lean your head to the right (without adding any special tension). Just note the naturally occurring tension on the sides of your neck as you do this. Hold for 5 seconds. Relax. Repeat the exercise leaning to the left. Then repeat leaning forward, bringing your chin toward your chest.

(Remember to keep breathing normally. And take your time – don't rush through these exercises!)

9. Raise your shoulders toward your ears (without adding any special tension). Hold for 5 seconds. Relax.

10. Shrug your shoulders; that is, bring them as far

forward and towards each other in front of your chest as you can. Hold for 5 seconds. Relax.

The next exercise is the *breath of relaxation*.

11. Take a deep breath by first expanding your stomach area, then mid-chest, and finally upper chest so that your lungs are filled to their maximum. Note the tension that occurs naturally in your upper body. Hold your breath for a count of 5 and exhale, letting loose in your neck, shoulders, upper arms and anywhere else that you noted any tension. Repeat this exercise with particular attention to 'letting go' as you exhale.

You can practise this exercise by itself, several times a day. With just a small amount of practice you will be able to 'let go' and relax any time you need to. Just take a deep breath, and consciously release tension in your upper body as you exhale. Apart from being an almost instantaneous release of tension, it clears your mind for a few moments of mental relaxation.

The next three exercises are for your mid-section.

12. Tense your stomach muscles as though to protect yourself from a blow to your middle. Hold for 5 seconds. Relax.

13. Press your back against your chair. Hold for 5 seconds. Relax.

14. Squeeze your buttocks together. Hold for 5 seconds. Relax.

The next set of three exercises is for your lower body.

15. Press your knees together. Hold for 5 seconds. Relax.

16. Press your heels down against the floor. Hold for 5 seconds. Relax.

17. Pull your toes back toward the soles of your feet. Hold for 5 seconds. Relax.

Finish the entire relaxation training routine by repeating the breath of relaxation twice. Then let your attention focus on the feeling in various parts of your body. Start with your head and work down. If you feel any residual tension in any part of your body, give that part a little wiggle, and consciously 'let go'.

Sit quietly for a few moments, breathe normally, and then open your eyes if they have been closed. You are ready to resume your regular daily activities.

With a couple of days' practice the sense of how your body feels when it is relaxed will be in your mind and under mental control. You will no longer need to tense your muscles before directing them to relax. Just take a deep breath and let go in whatever part of your body you felt any tension as you exhale. If you are like most people, you probably experience a certain amount of tension in your head, neck and shoulder regions, which, fortunately, are the regions most easily controlled and relaxed with the breath of relaxation exercise.

MEDITATION

Although there are a number of different forms of meditation, all focus on breathing and some relaxing mental procedure. Whichever specific way you choose can, with practice, have beneficial physical and mental effects, including the lowering of blood pressure, heart rate and respiration rate, as well as clearing of the mind.

Here is a simple but effective meditation technique that you can learn quickly and which I think will give you a great deal of satisfaction from the very first time you practise it.

Go to a quiet place where you can sit comfortably without being disturbed. Use an armchair if possible, so you can support your elbows and let your hands rest comfortably in your lap.

Close your eyes.

Check out your body.

If you feel any tension in your neck and shoulders, just rotate your head easily and slowly first in one direction, then the other, a couple of times. Wiggle your shoulders.

Focus on your breathing. Breathe slowly and naturally.

Quiet your mind by focusing in one of the following ways:

Pay attention only to the physical experience of breathing as you slowly inhale – that is, your chest expanding, the feeling of the air flowing in through your nostrils.

Make some sort of sound mentally, or repeat a word mentally, as you slowly exhale – for example, 'uhmmmm', the word 'one', or any other word, phrase or prayer that, because of its meaning in your life, has a calming effect.

Should outside thoughts intrude, as they probably will, especially when you first begin to practise meditation, just pull back and distance yourself from them. Simply 'notice them' as though they came from somewhere outside yourself. It's very important to stay quiet and relaxed, and never to feel that anything you experience while meditating is somehow 'wrong' or that you are not doing it 'right'. Even if you find yourself doing it many times, this act of putting yourself at a distance from any intrusion, becoming completely dispassionate no matter what your mind happens to do, and returning to your word or phrase and calm rhythmic breathing, is the key to experiencing the benefits of meditation.

If you spend about twenty minutes in meditation each day I think you will find that a feeling of calmness and of being in control will spread to other aspects of your life.

Here are some variations that you might enjoy in your meditation:

1. Count slowly to 4 as you breathe in and to a count of either 4 or 6 as you breathe out. Some people find it more relaxing to breathe out more slowly than in, but it's up to you to decide what feels best to you.

2. Instead of a word or counting as you breathe, just establish a calm rhythm, and simply 'listen'. Don't do anything but listen to all the sounds around you. Focus on your breathing and your ears. When thoughts intrude, as they will, do the distancing exercise and return to listening. This meditation approach involves different parts of the brain than when you repeat sounds to yourself (a word or phrase). I find this particularly relaxing.

3. 'Meditation in motion is superior to meditation at rest', according to one Oriental teacher of meditation. If you can walk or jog in a safe place where you don't have to pay attention to traffic, dogs or other distractions, get into a steady rhythm and count your steps as you breathe in and out (for example, 4 steps in, 4 steps out). Or simply switch into your 'listening' mode and listen to what's going on around you. It's important with meditation in motion only that you have a rhythm to your motion. I have known runners and swimmers who go into an almost trancelike state during activity, but you have to be able to do the activity easily and without paying it any attention.

With meditation in motion you obtain the benefits of two activities – you burn many extra calories and end up being greatly relaxed.

Appendix C

FAT AND CARBOHYDRATE COUNTER

Organization: the foods in this counter are listed alphabetically within the different categories mentioned below. Please remember that the figures given are for guidance only as the exact content of recipes and brands will always be subject to some variation.

T	=	*level* tablespoon
D	=	*level* dessertspoon
t	=	*level* teaspoon
scant t	=	level teaspoon with a little bit knocked off
Tr, ≤1, ≥	=	trace
1 cup	=	a measure of 8 fl oz / 225 ml
½ cup	=	a measure of 4 fl oz / 110 ml

	Serving	Total fat g	% Cal from fat	Carbs in g	Cal
Beverages					
apple juice	6 fl oz / 175 ml	0	0	21.8	87
beer					
regular*	12 fl oz / 350 ml	0	0	13.2	146
light*	12 fl oz / 350 ml	0	0	4.8	100
nonalcoholic	12 fl oz / 350 ml	0	0	14.1	70
carbonated drink					
regular	12 fl oz / 350 ml	0	0	38.5	151
sugar free	12 fl oz / 350 ml	0	0	0.3	2
coffee, brewed or instant	8 fl oz / 225 ml	0	0	1	5
daiquiri*	3.5 fl oz / 100 ml	0	0	7.2	194
eggnog, nonalcoholic, w/whole milk	8 fl oz / 225 ml	19.0	50	34.4	342
fruit punch	8 fl oz / 225 ml	0	0	29.4	116
Gatorade sports drink	8 fl oz / 225 ml	0	0	14.0	50
gin*	1 fl oz / 30 ml	0	0	0	73
grape juice drink	6 fl oz / 175 ml	0	0	24.2	94
lemonade	8 fl oz / 225 ml	0	0	26.9	102
lemonade, sugar-free	8 fl oz / 225 ml	0	0	1.3	5
orange juice, unsweetened	6 fl oz / 175 ml	0	0	19.1	23
pineapple-orange juice	6 fl oz / 175 ml	0	0	23	100
rum*	1 fl oz / 30 ml	0	0	0	65
soda water	12 fl oz / 350 ml	0	0	0	0
tea, brewed or instant	8 fl oz / 225 ml	0	0	0.4	2
tonic water	8 fl oz / 225 ml	0	0	21.4	83
vodka*	1 fl oz / 30 ml	0	0	0	65
whisky*	1 fl oz / 30 ml	0	0	0.6	70
wine*					
dessert and aperitif	4 fl oz / 110 ml	0	0	14.0	180
red or rosé	4 fl oz / 110 ml	0	0	0.9	85
white, dry or medium	4 fl oz / 110 ml	0	0	1.6	72
wine cooler	8 fl oz / 225 ml	0	0	2.0	143
Breads and Flours					
bagel, cinnamon raisin	1 medium	2.0	8	48.0	240
bagel, plain	1 medium	1.4	8	30.9	163
bread					
cracked wheat	1 slice	0.9	12	12.5	66

*Although alcohol contains no fat, scientific evidence suggests that it may facilitate fat storage and hamper your weight-loss efforts. Excessive alcohol intake is detrimental to your health. We concur with other health organizations in recommending discretion in the use of alcoholic beverages.

	Serving	Total fat g	% Cal from fat	Carbs in g	Cal
French/Vienna	1 slice	1.0	13	12.6	70
fruit loaf	1 slice	1	n/a	13.2	70
granary	1 slice	1.3	n/a	23.1	128
honey wheatberry	1 slice	1.0	13	13.0	70
Hovis	1 slice	1.0	n/a	20.8	106
Italian	1 slice	0.6	7	14.9	78
mixed grain	1 slice	0.9	13	11.7	64
pitta, plain	1 large	0.8	3	46.8	240
pitta, wholemeal	1 large	1.2	4	44.8	236
rye	1 slice	0.9	12	12.0	66
rye, pumpernickel	1 slice	0.8	9	15.4	82
sourdough	1 slice	1.0	13	12.0	70
white, commercial	1 slice	1.0	13	13.0	70
white, hmde	1 slice	1.7	21	12.0	72
white, 'lite'	1 slice	0.5	11	9.6	42
wholemeal, commercial	1 slice	1.0	13	12.0	70
breadcrumbs	1 cup	4.6	11	73.4	392
breadsticks					
plain	1 small	0.3	7	7.5	39
sesame	1 small	2.2	39	6.3	51
bulgur wheat, dry	1 cup	1.9	4	106.2	479
cornmeal, dry	5½ oz / 150 g	2.2	4	107.0	585
cornflour	1D	0	0	7.3	31
cream crackers					
regular	1 cracker	0.6	n/a	5.2	32
brown wheat	1 cracker	1.3	n/a	4.7	32
choice grain	1 cracker	1.0	n/a	4.9	29
crispbreads					
graham	2 squares	1.5	23	10.8	60
graham, crumbs	½ cup	4.0	15	44.0	240
matzohs	1 board	1.9	15	22.0	115
melba toast	1 piece	0.1	6	6.9	15
oyster	33 crackers	3.3	27	17.5	109
rice cakes	1 piece	0.2	5	8.0	35
Ritz	3 crackers	3.0	9	6.7	53
Ritz cheese	3 crackers	2.5	5.6	3.5	40
Ryvita, darkrye	2 crackers	0.4	n/a	11.2	50
Ryvita, plain	2 crackers	0.4	n/a	11.0	50
Ryvita, sesame	2 crackers	1.4	n/a	12.0	60
saltines	2 crackers	0.6	21	4.4	26
sesame wafers	3 crackers	3.0	39	9.5	70
soda	5 crackers	1.9	27	10.0	63

	Serving	Total fat g	% Cal from fat	Carbs in g	Cal
wholemeal bran	2 biscuits	5.8	n/a	16.8	128
croissant	1 small	7.0	37	22.0	170
croutons, commercial	3T	2.2	34	8.5	59
crumpets, w/out butter	1	0.3	n/a	17.4	83
Danish pastry	1 medium	14.0	47	34.0	270
doughnut	1 2.2 oz / 60 g	13.7	49	29.7	234
flour					
buckwheat	4 oz / 110 g	2.5	7	70.6	326
rice	4 oz / 110 g	0.9	2	91.0	398
rye	4 oz / 110 g	2.2	5	81.0	400
soya	3½ oz / 100 g	18.6	45	25.8	373
white, cake	3½ oz / 100 g	0.9	2	93.7	436
white, plain	3½ oz / 100 g	1.4	3	04.3	499
white, bread	3½ oz / 100 g	3.0	7	79.5	401
white, self-raising	3½ oz / 100 g	1.2	2	94.4	436
wholemeal	3½ oz / 100 g	2.4	5	85.2	400
French toast, hmde	1 slice	6.7	39	17.2	153
muffins					
all types; commercial	1 large (3 oz / 80 g)	10.3	38	27.2	242
banana nut	1 large (4 oz / 110 g)	15.8	38	52.2	371
bran, hmde	1 medium	5.1	41	16.7	112
corn	1 medium	4.2	29	20.0	130
pancakes, English style	2 pancakes	8.1	n/a	35.0	301
pastry					
flaky	1¾ oz / 50 g	20.3	n/a	23.7	283
shortcrust	1¾ oz / 50 g	16.1	n/a	27.8	264
rolls					
crescent	1	5.6	50	11.1	100
croissant	1 small	6.0	45	13.0	120
French	1	0.4	3	28.3	137
hamburger	1	2.1	17	20.1	114
hard	1	1.0	9	19.0	100
hot dog	1	2.1	17	20.1	114
sesame seed	1	1.0	15	11.0	60
submarine	1 medium	2.0	5	72.0	360
wheat	1	0.8	10	14.6	72
white, commercial	1	2.0	23	14.0	80
white, hmde	1	2.0	20	13.0	89
whole wheat	1	0.8	10	14.6	72
scones, hmde	1¾ oz / 50 g	7.3	n/a	28.0	186

	Serving	Total fat g	% Cal from fat	Carbs in g	Cal
Scotch pancakes	1¾ oz / 50 g	5.8	n/a	20.3	142
stuffing					
bread, from mix	½ cup	12.8	55	19.7	208
sweet roll, iced	1 medium	6.8	40	21.4	154
tortilla					
corn (unfried)	1 medium	1.1	15	12.8	67
flour	1 medium	2.0	21	15.0	85
turnover, fruit filled	1	7.8	41	23.4	173
waffle, hmde	1 large	12.6	46	27.7	245
Cereals					
All Bran	1½ oz / 40 g	1.4	n/a	18.4	109
bran 100%	½ cup	1.4	17	20.7	76
bran, unprocessed, dry	¼ cup	0.6	17	9.7	32
Bran Buds	1½ oz / 40 g	1.2	n/a	20.0	112
Bran Flakes	1¾ oz / 50 g	1.0	n/a	31.5	160
Cheerios, multi	1½ oz / 40 g	1.5	n/a	30.4	148
Coco Pops	1½ oz / 40 g	0.4	n/a	34.8	152
cornflakes	1½ oz / 40 g	0.6	n/a	34.0	147
Frosties	1½ oz / 40 g	0.2	n/a	35.2	152
Fruit & Fibre	1½ oz / 40 g	2.4	n/a	26.8	140
w/dates, raisins, walnuts	⅔ cup	2.0	15	27.0	120
Golden Grahams	1½ oz / 40 g	1.4	n/a	3x2.6	152
Grapenuts	1½ oz / 40 g	1.2	n/a	30.4	142
Muesli, Co-op Good Life w/o sugar	1¾ oz / 50 g	1.7	n/a	33.2	167
oat bran flakes	1¾ oz / 50 g	2.5	n/a	32.0	175
oat bran with raisins and apple	1¾ oz / 50 g	2.3	n/a	65.0	340
oats, Ready Brek, dry weight	1 oz / 28 g	2.4	n/a	19.6	109
Pop Tarts, apple	2 oz / 52 g	7	n/a	34.0	210
porridge, hmde	3½ oz / 100 g	0.9	n/a	8.2	44
puffed wheat	1¾ oz / 50 g	0.7	n/a	34.3	163
Rice Krispies	1¾ oz / 50 g	1.0	n/a	44.1	186
Shredded Wheat	2 pieces	1.05	n/a	31.9	157
Special K	1¾ oz / 50 g	1.3	n/a	39.1	199
Sugar Puffs	1¾ oz / 50 g	0.4	n/a	42.3	174
Weetabix	1¾ oz / 50 g	1.7	n/a	35.2	170
Wheat Bisks	2 biscuits	1.0	n/a	26.0	130
wheat germ, toasted	3T	2.8	24	14.9	104
Wholegrain Feast	1½ oz / 40 g	3.8	n/a	26.0	154
Cheeses					
blue	1 oz / 28 g	8.2	74	0.7	100

	Serving	Total fat g	% Cal from fat	Carbs in g	Cal
Brie	1 oz / 28 g	7.9	75	0.1	95
Cheddar					
grated	3T	9.4	74	0.4	114
sliced	1 oz / 28 g	9.4	74	0.4	114
Cheddarie	1 oz / 28 g	5.9	n/a	2.0	78
Cheddarie Light	1 oz / 28 g	4.2	n/a	2.8	67
cheese spread (Kraft)	1 oz / 28 g	6.0	66	2.5	82
cottage cheese					
very low fat	4 oz / 110 g	1.2	13	3.1	82
regular	4 oz / 110 g	2.2	20	4.1	101
w/added cream	4 oz / 110 g	5.1	39	3.0	117
cream cheese	2D	9.9	90	0.8	99
Edam	1 oz / 28 g	7.9	70	0.4	101
feta	1 oz / 28 g	6.0	72	1.2	75
fromage fraîs	1 oz / 28 g	2.2	n/a	1.2	34
Gouda	1 oz / 28 g	7.8	70	0.6	101
Jarlsberg	1 oz / 28 g	7.0	63	1.0	100
Kraft Singles	1 oz / 28 g	7.5	75	3.0	90
Kraft Light Singles	1 oz / 28 g	4.0	51	2.0	70
mozzarella					
partly skimmed	1 oz / 28 g	4.5	56	0.8	72
whole milk	1 oz / 28 g	6.1	69	0.6	80
Parmesan					
grated	1D	1.5	59	0.2	23
hard	1 oz / 28 g	7.3	59	0.9	111
ricotta					
partly skimmed	4 oz / 110 g	9.8	52	6.4	171
whole milk	4 oz / 110 g	16.1	67	3.8	216
Roquefort	1 oz / 28 g	8.7	75	0.6	105
Shape 15%	1 oz / 28 g	4.6	n/a	0.1	73
Shape 14% mature	1 oz / 28 g	4.4	n/a	Tr	73
Stilton	1 oz / 28 g	11.2	n/a	Tr	129
Combination Foods					
baked beans w/pork	½ cup	2.0	14	25.2	133
beans & franks, tinned	1 cup	16.8	42	39.4	364
beans, refried, tinned	½ cup	1.4	10	23.3	134
beef & vegetable stew	1 cup	10.5	43	15.2	218
beef ribs w/gravy, frzn	5¾ oz / 170 g	20.0	52	12.0	350
beef stew, tinned	1 cup	7.0	30	15.0	207
casserole, meat, veg., rice, sauce	1 cup	17.0	43	29.0	360
cauliflower cheese, hmde	7 oz / 200 g	16.0	n/a	9.8	226

	Serving	Total fat g	% Cal from fat	Carbs in g	Cal
cheese soufflé	1 cup	16.2	70	5.9	207
Chicken Cajun, Weight Watchers	14 oz / 400 g	10.6	n/a	51.4	371
chicken à l'orange, Lean Cuisine	9½ oz / 252 g	4.7	n/a	34.6	276
chicken à la king, hmde	1 cup	34.3	66	12.3	468
chicken & dumplings	1 cup	10.4	38	16.0	248
chicken & rice casserole	1 cup	17.0	43	29.0	360
chicken fricassee, hmde	1 cup	22.3	52	7.4	386
chicken noodle casserole	1 cup	15.0	44	21.0	310
chicken parmigiana, hmde	7 oz / 200 g	14.8	43	22.7	308
chicken salad, regular	½ cup	20.0	70	12.0	256
chicken tetrazzini	1 cup	19.6	49	28.0	360
chilli					
con carne with rice,					
Weight Watchers	14 oz / 400 g	5.6	n/a	56.1	352
w/beans	1 cup	14.0	44	30.4	286
w/o beans	1 cup	33.5	73	12.1	412
chop suey w/o rice					
beef	1 cup	17.0	51	13.0	300
fish or poultry	1 cup	4.0	26	7.0	141
chow mein, chicken, hmde	1 cup	10.0	35	10.0	255
corned-beef hash	1 cup	24.0	60	19.0	360
devilled crab	½ cup	12.0	45	25.0	240
devilled egg	1 large	5.3	76	0	63
egg foo yung w/sauce	1 piece	3.5	39	9.5	80
egg salad	½ cup	23.0	78	4.0	267
egg roll, restaurant	1 (3½ oz / 100 g)	6.0	30	23.0	180
enchilada, bean, beef & cheese	1 piece	13.0	43	28.0	270
fish pie, hmde	10 oz / 300 g	17.1	n/a	39.0	384
fisherman's pie, Lean Cuisine	11 oz / 320 g	5.6	n/a	32.7	265
fritter, corn	1 medium	7.5	51	13.9	132
green pepper stuffed w/rice & beef	1 average	11.0	44	18.0	225
ham salad w/mayo	½ cup	18.4	64	12.8	259
Irish stew, hmde	7 oz / 200 g	14.6	n/a	20.2	248
lasagna, hmde w/beef & cheese	1 piece	17.0	38	38.0	400
lobster					
Newburg	½ cup	13.3	49	16.4	243
salad	½ cup	8.5	53	4.9	145
macaroni cheese, hmde	5½ oz / 150 g	14.6	n/a	22.6	261
meatball (reg. beef)	1 medium	4.3	60	2.5	72
meat loaf, w/reg. beef	3½ oz / 100 g	20.4	55	10.8	332
moussaka, hmde	7 oz / 200 g	26.8	n/a	19.6	390
onion rings	10 average	16.0	58	22.0	250

	Serving	Total fat g	% Cal from fat	Carbs in g	Cal
oysters Rockefeller, traditional	6–8 oysters	14.3	58	13.2	223
pasta sauce, Ragu	3½ oz / 100 g	2.8	n/a	12.1	79
pizza					
cheese	1 slice	9.5	46	16.5	185
cheese, French bread, frzn	5⅛ oz / 150 g	13.0	34	41.0	340
combination w/meat	1 slice	15.0	50	23.0	269
deep dish, cheese	1 slice	13.5	29	49.0	426
pepperoni, frzn	¼ pizza	21.3	52	29.2	368
pork, sweet & sour, w/rice	1 cup	7.5	25	52.3	270
pork pie	3½ oz / 100 g	27.0	n/a	24.9	376
quiche					
Lorraine (bacon)	⅛ pie	41.0	68	31.0	540
plain or vegetable	1 slice	17.6	51	45.0	312
sandwiches					
BLT w/mayo	1	17.0	44	26.0	347
chicken w/mayo & lettuce	1	14.4	43	23.0	303
club w/mayo	1	20.8	32	41.7	590
corned beef on rye	1	12.0	38	26.0	286
cream cheese & jam	1	22.0	52	35.2	380
egg salad	1	14.0	45	28.0	281
grilled cheese	1	29.0	59	26.0	443
ham, cheese & mayo	1	15.5	39	33.3	353
ham salad	1	13.6	38	36.0	322
peanut butter & jam	1	16.0	39	44.0	368
roast beef & mayo	1	20.0	43	26.0	418
sub w/salami & cheese	1	41.0	44	88.0	833
tuna salad	1	21.0	48	29.0	396
turkey & mayo	1	18.4	41	27.6	402
turkey breast & mustard	1	5.2	16	27.6	285
turkey ham on rye	1	9.0	34	23.0	239
scotch egg, hmde	3½ oz / 100g	20.9	n/a	11.8	558
shrimp or prawn salad	½ cup	9.0	60	6.0	135
spaghetti					
tinned	7½ oz / 200 g	0.8	n/a	27.2	124
tinned, Weight Watchers	7½ oz / 200 g	0.8	n/a	20.2	102
w/meat sauce	1 cup	11.7	31	38.7	332
w/tomato sauce	1 cup	8.8	31	37.0	260
spinach soufflé	1 cup	18.4	76	2.8	218
sushi w/fish & vegetables	5 oz / 145 g	1.0	6	17.0	141
tortellini, meat or cheese	1 cup	8.0	19	55.0	370
tostada w/refried beans	1 medium	11.0	41	27.0	243
tuna noodle casserole	1 cup	13.0	38	31.0	310

	Serving	Total fat g	% Cal from fat	Carbs in g	Cal
tuna salad					
oil pack, w/mayo	½ cup	16.3	65	7.7	226
water pack, w/mayo	½ cup	10.5	55	7.7	170
veal parmigiana, hmde	1 cup	22.0	49	34.0	400
veal scallopini	1 cup	19.0	42	14.0	412
vegetable curry w/rice,					
Menu Masters	12 oz / 354 g	17.0	n/a	68.0	460
Welsh rarebit, w/buttered toast	7 oz / 200 g	47.2	n/a	47.8	730

Desserts, Ice Creams and Toppings

	Serving	Total fat g	% Cal from fat	Carbs in g	Cal
Angel Delight,					
butterscotch with skimmed milk	per serving	3.1	n/a	11.0	84
apple crumble, hmde	3½ oz / 100 g	T	n/a	17.2	160
baklava	1 piece	16.0	49	35.0	295
brownie, choc., plain	1 small	5.0	43	15.0	105
cake					
angel food	1/12 cake	0.1	1	35.7	161
banana w/frosting	1/12 cake	18.0	39	60.0	410
butter w/frosting	1/12 cake	18.0	51	61.0	320
carrot w/frosting	1/12 cake	18.0	39	59.0	410
choc. w/frosting	1/12 cake	19.0	41	58.0	420
coconut w/frosting	1/12 cake	18.1	41	54.3	395
fancy iced	1¾ oz / 50 g	7.5	n/a	34.4	204
fruit, rich w/o icing	1¾ oz / 50 g	5.6	n/a	29.2	166
gingerbread	1¾ oz / 50 g	6.3	n/a	31.4	187
lemon w/frosting	1/12 cake	18.0	39	60.0	420
madeira	1¾ oz / 50 g	8.5	n/a	29.2	196
pound	1/12 cake	9.0	41	28.0	200
spice w/frosting	1/12 cake	18.0	39	36.0	420
sponge, w/out fat	1 piece	3.1	15	35.7	188
streusel swirl	1/12 cake	11.0	38	37.7	260
cereal bar, average	1½ oz / 40 g	8.8	n/a	19.9	164
cheesecake, traditional	1/8 pie	16.3	57	24.3	257
cookies & biscuits					
choc., Homewheat	1	4.1	n/a	10.7	69
choc., Rich Tea	1	2.7	n/a	8.7	62
choc. chip, hmde	1	2.7	53	6.4	46
custard cream	1	2.8	n/a	7.8	59
digestive, Light	1	1.1	n/a	10.7	69
digestive, sweetmeal	1	3.4	n/a	9.8	74
Hovis digestive	1	2.7	n/a	7.9	57
fig bar	1	1.0	17	10.6	53

	Serving	Total fat g	% Cal from fat	Carbs in g	Cal
gingernuts	1	1.7	n/a	7.5	47
graham cracker, choc. covered	1	2.0	40	5.5	45
macaroon, coconut	1	3.4	51	6.6	60
vanilla-creme sandwich	1	2.0	36	7.0	50
vanilla wafers	3	2.0	30	11.0	60
Weight Watchers					
stem ginger cookies	2	3.1	n/a	14.8	92
cream puff w/custard	1	18.1	54	26.7	303
cupcake					
choc. w/icing	1	6.0	31	28.4	172
yellow w/icing	1	5.0	28	27.0	160
custard, baked	½ cup	6.6	40	15.1	148
date bar	1 bar	2.0	20	6.0	90
éclair w/choc. icing & cream, hmde	1¾ oz / 50 g	12.0	n/a	19.1	188
fruit ice/sorbet	½ cup	0	0	29.0	120
fruitcake	1 piece	6.6	36	25.7	163
fruit pie, individ.	3½ oz / 100 g	15.5	n/a	56.7	369
ice cream					
Bird's Eye lowfat superwhip	3½ fl oz / 100 ml	8.7	n/a	10.0	124
choc. ice	2½ oz / 70 g	12.8	n/a	18.9	200
Cornetto	1	11.9	n/a	24.5	218
fruit ice, Calippo	1	0	n/a	26.1	107
sorbet	½ cup	0	0	29.0	120
vanilla, regular	3½ oz / 100 g	6.6	n/a	20.0	156
vanilla, luxury	3½ oz / 100 g	15.6	n/a	21.6	244
Walls almond magnum	4 fl oz / 110 ml	22.4	n/a	26.5	329
ice cream cone (cone only)	1 medium	0.3	6	9.3	45
ice milk					
Friji choc. shake	7 fl oz / 200 ml	3.6	n/a	23.0	158
Ski low fat yog. drink	7 fl oz / 200 ml	0.6	n/a	29.8	142
jelly, made up	1¾ oz / 50 g	0	n/a	7.1	30
meringues, hmde w/out cream	1¾ oz / 50 g	0	n/a	47.8	190
mousse, choc., hmde	½ cup	32.9	66	33.2	447
pie					
fruit w/pastry top, hmde	3½ oz / 100 g	15.6	n/a	56.8	370
lemon meringue, hmde	3½ oz / 100 g	14.6	n/a	46.4	324
mincemeat, hmde	1¾ oz / 50 g	10.4	n/a	30.9	218
pecan	⅛ pie	23.6	50	52.8	431
pumpkin	⅛ pie	12.8	48	27.9	241
Popsicle	1 bar	0	0	20.0	80
pudding					
bread & butter	3½ oz / 100 g	7.8	n/a	17.2	159

	Serving	Total fat g	% Cal from fat	Carbs in g	Cal
Christmas	3½ oz / 100 g	11.6	n/a	47.6	304
queen of	3½ oz / 100 g	7.9	n/a	33.5	216
rice	½ cup	4.1	21	30.0	175
tapioca	½ cup	4.1	23	27.6	161
sorbet	3½ oz / 100 g	0	n/a	26.0	98
toppings					
butterscotch/caramel	3D	0.1	<1.0	27.0	155
choc. fudge	2D	4.0	33	18.0	110
crème fraîche	1 oz / 28 g	4.2	n/a	1.4	48
pecans in syrup	3D	1.5	7	42.0	195
pineapple	3D	0.2	1	36.0	150
single cream	1 oz / 28 g	5.9	n/a	0.9	59
strawberry	3D	0	0	42.0	150
whipping cream					
double, unwhipped	1D	5.6	97	0.4	52
whipping, unwhipped	1D	4.6	94	0.4	44
treacle tart, hmde	3½ oz / 100 g	14.0	n/a	61.4	186
trifle, hmde	3½ oz / 100 g	6.2	n/a	24.4	160
turnover, fruit filled	1	7.9	47	23.2	173
yoghurt, frozen, low fat	½ cup	1.0	7	23.0	120
Eggs					
boiled/poached	1	5.0	61	0.6	74
fried w/½ t fat	1 large	7.0	70	0.6	91
omelette					
2 oz / 56 g cheese, 3 egg	1	41.0	71	2.6	516
plain, 3 egg	1	22.2	69	1.8	289
Spanish, 2 egg	1	17.2	61	7.2	254
scrambled w/milk	1 large	7.5	67	1.3	101
white	1 large	0	0	0.3	17
yolk	1 large	5.1	78	0.3	59

Fast Foods / Restaurants
(all listings are for standard servings for the given establishment unless otherwise noted)

Burger King					
apple pie	1	14.0	n/a	45.0	320
bacon double cheeseburger	1	33.8	n/a	29.4	545
BK flamer	1	16.8	n/a	26.0	344
BK spicy beanburger	1	22.8	n/a	68.6	545
cheeseburger	1	16.5	n/a	31.1	337
cheeseburger deluxe	1	21.8	n/a	31.5	390

	Serving	Total fat g	% Cal from fat	Carbs in g	Cal
cheeseburger, double	1	30.9	n/a	32.4	521
chicken royale	1	27.7	n/a	51.7	557
chicken pick 'em ups	6 pieces	9.7	n/a	16.0	219
croissan'wich	1	26.3	n/a	23.4	402
croissan'wich w/bacon	1	29.4	n/a	23.5	442
croissan'wich w/ham	1	27.0	n/a	24.8	560
french fries, regular	1 order	17.4	n/a	44.1	352
hamburger	1	10.7	n/a	29.8	265
mushroom double Swiss	1	31.3	n/a	29.4	510
oatbran w/bacon	1	21.1	n/a	27.6	379
oatbran w/egg & cheese	1	18.0	n/a	27.5	339
oatbran w/ham	1	18.7	n/a	28.9	497
ocean catch	1	11.1	n/a	42.1	342
onion rings	1	13.1	n/a	26.8	231
shakes					
chocolate, small	1	6.1	n/a	58.8	323
strawberry, small	1	5.8	n/a	57.2	314
vanilla, small	1	5.6	n/a	51.4	292
whopper	1	29.8	n/a	47.3	560
whopper w/cheese	1	41.4	n/a	49.9	703
whopper, double	1	46.1	n/a	47.3	780
whopper, double w/cheese	1	57.7	n/a	49.9	923
Kentucky Fried Chicken (KFC)					
apple pie	1	15.2	n/a	28.5	250
barbeque beans	1	2.2	n/a	40.5	224
chicken, original recipe	1	14.3	n/a	4.6	210
coleslaw, regular	1	8.2	n/a	10.4	119
Colonel's classic burger	1	20.2	n/a	40.3	420
Colonel's fillet burger	1	15.9	n/a	36.7	386
corn salad, regular	1	7.4	n/a	17.6	149
corn-on-the-cob	1 order	5.5	n/a	43.9	244
fries, regular	1 order	12.7	n/a	42.4	295
Kentucky dippers	5 pieces	20.7	n/a	15.1	322
hot wings	5 pieces	17.2	n/a	11.1	409
zinger	1	22.3	n/a	34.9	447
McDonald's					
apple pie	1	13.8	n/a	21.4	219
bacon & egg McMuffin	1	16.1	n/a	26.9	333
Big Mac	1	26.2	n/a	36.7	486
cheeseburger	1	13.3	n/a	28.0	300
chicken McNuggets	6 pieces	13.9	n/a	16.9	266
donut, plain	1	16.3	n/a	29.7	282

	Serving	Total fat g	% Cal from fat	Carbs in g	Cal
donut, chocolate	1	17.6	n/a	32.0	300
filet-o-fish	1	15.8	n/a	36.1	350
french fries, regular	1 order	14.3	n/a	31.2	267
hamburger	1	8.6	n/a	27.7	244
hashbrown	1 order	7.8	n/a	15.1	135
McChicken sandwich	1	15.8	n/a	38.6	370
pizza, cheese & tomato	1	28.6	n/a	51.7	573
pizza, pepperoni	1	34.2	n/a	66.1	666
pizza, deluxe	1	32.0	n/a	61.4	652
quarter pounder	1	22.0	n/a	29.7	411
quarter pounder w/cheese	1	27.7	n/a	33.7	501
salad, side	1	4.6	n/a	1.7	74
sausage & egg McMuffin	1	26.1	n/a	24.6	427
scrambled eggs & muffin w/butter	1	9.4	n/a	30.4	280
shakes					
banana, regular	1	7.0	n/a	73.7	396
chocolate, regular	1	7.0	n/a	66.4	365
strawberry, regular	1	7.0	n/a	69.3	377
vanilla, regular	1	7.0	n/a	66.0	364

Fats

	Serving	Total fat g	% Cal from fat	Carbs in g	Cal
bacon fat	1D	14.0	100	0	126
beef, separable fat	1 oz / 28 g	23.3	100	0	210
butter					
solid	1 scant t	4.0	100	0	36
solid	1D	12.0	100	0	108
chicken fat, raw	1D	12.8	100	0	115
cream					
double	1D	5.6	97	0.4	52
light	1D	2.9	90	0.6	29
medium (25% fat)	1D	3.8	92	0.5	37
cream substitute					
liquid	1T	1.5	67	1.7	20
powdered	1 scant t	0.7	57	1.1	11
crème fraîche 15%	1 oz / 28 g	4.2	n/a	1.4	48
margarine					
low fat	1 scant t	2.0	100	0	18
regular	1 scant t	4.0	100	0	36
mayonnaise					
reduced calorie	1D	5.0	90	1.0	50
regular (soybean)	1D	11.0	100	0.4	100
oil					

	Serving	Total fat g	% Cal from fat	Carbs in g	Cal
corn	1D	13.3	100	0	120
olive	1D	13.3	100	0	119
safflower	1D	13.3	100	0	120
soybean	1D	13.3	100	0	120
pork, separable fat, cooked	1 oz / 28 g	24.0	100	0	216
pork fat (lard)	1D	12.8	100	0	116
salt pork, raw	1 oz / 28 g	23.8	98	0	219
shortening, vegetable	1D	12.0	n/a	0	108
sour cream	1T	2.5	86	0.5	26

Fish
(all baked/ steamed/grilled w/o added fat unless otherwise noted)

	Serving	Total fat g	% Cal from fat	Carbs in g	Cal
anchovy, tinned	3 fillets	1.1	40	0	25
anchovy paste	1 scant t	0.8	51	0.5	14
bass					
saltwater, black	3½ oz / 100 g	1.2	12	0	93
seabass, white	3½ oz / 100 g	2.5	21	0	105
bluefish					
cooked	3½ oz / 100 g	5.36	31	0	157
fried	3½ oz / 100 g	12.8	56	6.5	205
carp	3½ oz / 100 g	6.1	40	0	138
catfish	3½ oz / 100 g	3.1	27	0	103
catfish, breaded & fried	3½ oz / 100 g	13.2	53	6.8	226
caviar, black or red, granular	1 round t	1.0	69	0.2	13
clams					
tinned, solids & liquid	½ cup	0.7	7	3.0	85
tinned, solids only	3 oz / 80 g	1.6	12	4.1	118
meat only	5 large	1.0	13	2.5	67
soft, raw	4 large	0.8	11	2.2	63
cod					
cooked	3½ oz / 100 g	0.8	7	0	104
dried, salted	3½ oz / 100 g	2.3	7	0	287
crab					
tinned	½ cup	0.9	12	0	67
devilled	3½ oz / 100 g	10.1	42	22.6	217
crayfish, freshwater	3½ oz / 100 g	1.4	11	0	113
eel					
stewed	3½ oz / 100 g	18.3	63	0	260
smoked	3½ oz / 100 g	23.6	75	0	281
fillets, frzn					
batter dipped	2 pieces	25.8	52	37.6	447
light & crispy	2 pieces	15.9	48	27.3	301

	Serving	Total fat g	% Cal from fat	Carbs in g	Cal
fish cakes, frzn, fried	3½ oz / 100 g	8.8	44	22.7	181
fish fingers, frzn, fried	3½ oz / 100 g	12.7	n/a	17.2	233
flatfish	3½ oz / 100 g	0.8	9	0	79
flounder/sole	3½ oz / 100 g	0.5	7	0	68
gefilte fish	3½ oz / 100 g	1.7	18	7.4	84
grouper	3½ oz / 100 g	1.3	1	0	117
haddock					
steamed	3½ oz / 100 g	0.6	7	0	79
fried	3½ oz / 100 g	14.2	45	25.6	284
halibut	3½ oz / 100 g	1.2	11	0	100
herring					
fillet, grilled	3½ oz / 100 g	13.0	n/a	0	199
pickled	3½ oz / 100 g	17.9	62	9.6	260
kipper, fillet, baked	3½ oz / 100 g	11.4	n/a	0	205
lobster, northern					
grilled w/fat	12 oz / 350 g	15.1	31	4.5	445
boiled	3½ oz / 100 g	0.6	5	1.33	97
mackerel	3½ oz / 100 g	12.2	57	0	191
mussels					
tinned	3½ oz / 100 g	4.5	25	7.4	163
meat only	3½ oz / 100 g	2.1	23	3.5	84
octopus	3½ oz / 100 g	2.1	11	4.3	163
oysters					
tinned	3½ oz / 100 g	2.5	33	3.6	68
fried	3½ oz / 100 g	12.5	58	11.6	195
raw	5–8 medium	2.1	33	3.3	58
perch, freshwater, yellow	3½ oz / 100 g	0.9	9	0	91
pike					
blue	3½ oz / 100 g	0.9	9	0	90
northern	3½ oz / 100 g	1.1	11	0	88
walleye	3½ oz / 100 g	1.2	12	0	93
pollock, Atlantic	3½ oz / 100 g	1.0	10	0	91
pompano	3½ oz / 100 g	9.5	52	0	166
prawns					
tinned, drained	3½ oz / 100 g	1.6	14	0.9	102
fried	3½ oz / 100 g	12.2	46	11.5	240
raw or boiled	3½ oz / 100 g	1.8	15	0.8	105
red snapper	3½ oz / 100 g	1.9	18	0	93
rockfish, oven steamed	3½ oz / 100 g	2.5	21	0	107
roe					
cod, hard, fried	3½ oz / 100 g	11.9	n/a	3.0	202
herring, soft, fried	3½ oz / 100 g	15.8	n/a	4.7	244

	Serving	Total fat g	% Cal from fat	Carbs in g	Cal
salmon					
Atlantic	3½ oz / 100 g	6.3	40	0	141
grilled/baked	3½ oz / 100 g	7.4	37	0	182
pink, tinned	3½ oz / 100 g	5.1	39	0	118
smoked	3½ oz / 100 g	9.3	47	0	176
sardines					
Atlantic, in soy oil	2 sardines	2.8	50	0	50
Pacific, in tomato sauce	2 sardines	9.2	61	1	136
scallops					
cooked	3½ oz / 100 g	0.7	7	2.5	88
frzn, fried	3½ oz / 100 g	10.9	45	10.1	214
steamed	3½ oz / 100 g	0.7	7	2.5	88
sea bass, white	3½ oz / 100 g	1.5	14	0	96
smelt, tinned	4–5 medium	13.5	61	0	200
sole, fillet	3½ oz / 100 g	0.5	7	0	68
squid					
fried	3 oz / 80 g	6.4	39	6.6	149
raw	3 oz / 80 g	1.2	14	2.6	78
swordfish	3½ oz / 100 g	5.2	30	0	154
trout					
brown w/bones	3½ oz / 100 g	2.1	19	0	101
rainbow, fried	3½ oz / 100 g	11.4	53	0	195
tuna					
albacore, raw	3½ oz / 100 g	7.5	38	0	177
bluefin, raw	3½ oz / 100 g	4.1	25	0	145
tinned, skipjack in oil, drained	3½ oz / 100 g	8.0	39	0	185
tinned, skipjack in brine, drained	3½ oz / 100 g	2.4	16	0	135
yellowfin, raw	3½ oz / 100 g	3.0	20	0	133
whitebait, fried	3½ oz / 100 g	47.5	n/a	5.3	525
whiting	3½ oz / 100 g	1.7	13	0	114
winkles, boiled, shelled	3½ oz / 100 g	1.4	n/a	Tr	74
Fruit					
apple					
dried	½ cup	0.1	1	28.3	105
whole w/peel	1 medium	0.5	5	21.1	81
stewed, unsweetened	½ cup	0.1	2	13.8	53
apricots					
dried	10 halves	0.2	2	21.6	83
fresh	3 medium	0.4	7	11.8	51
avocado					
California	1 (6 oz / 175 g)	30.0	88	12.0	306

	Serving	Total fat g	% Cal from fat	Carbs in g	Cal
Florida	1(11 oz / 325 g)	27.0	72	27.1	339
banana	1 medium	0.6	5	26.7	105
banana chips	½ cup	8.0	29	15.0	248
blackberries					
fresh	1 cup	0.6	7	18.4	74
frzn, unsweetened	1 cup	0.7	7	23.7	97
blueberries					
fresh	1 cup	0.6	7	20.5	82
frzn, unsweetened	1 cup	1.0	11	18.8	78
boysenberries, frzn, unsweetened	1 cup	0.4	5	16.1	66
breadfruit, fresh	¼ small	0.2	2	26.0	99
cantaloupe	½ small	0.4	6	13.4	57
cherries					
maraschino	3T	0.2	3	16.6	66
tinned, in heavy syrup	½ cup	0.1	1	29.8	116
sweet	½ cup	0.7	13	11.3	49
cranberries, fresh	1 cup	0.2	4	12.1	46
cranberry sauce	½ cup	0.2	1	53.7	209
dates, whole dried	10 dates	0.4	1	61.0	228
figs					
tinned	3 figs	0.1	1	19.5	75
dried, uncooked	10 figs	2.2	4	122.2	477
fresh	1 medium	0.2	5	9.6	37
fruit cocktail, tinned w/juice	1 cup	0.3	2	29.4	112
grapefruit					
fresh	½ medium	0.1	2	9.5	37
tinned in syrup	3½ oz / 100 g	Tr	n/a	15.5	60
grapes, Thompson seedless	3 oz / 80 g	0.1	1	25.2	94
guava, fresh	1 medium	0.5	1	10.7	45
honeydew melon, fresh	¼ small	0.1	2	11.8	46
kiwi fruit, fresh	1 medium	0.3	6	11.3	46
kumquat, fresh	1 medium	0	0	3.1	12
lemon, fresh	1 medium	0.2	11	5.4	17
lime, fresh	1 medium	0.1	5	7.1	20
mandarin oranges, tinned w/juice	½ cup	0	0	11.9	46
mango, fresh	1 medium	0.6	4	35.2	135
melon, honeydew	3½ oz / 100 g	Tr	n/a	5.0	21
mixed fruit, dried	½ cup	0.5	2	64.1	243
nectarine, fresh	1 medium	0.6	8	16.0	67
orange					
naval, fresh	1 medium	0.1	1	16.3	65
Valencia, fresh	1 medium	0.4	6	14.4	59

	Serving	Total fat g	% Cal from fat	Carbs in g	Cal
papaya, fresh	1 medium	0.4	3	29.8	117
passionfruit, purple, fresh	1 medium	0.1	5	4.2	18
peach					
tinned in heavy syrup	1 cup	0.3	1	51.0	190
tinned in light syrup	1 cup	0.1	1	36.5	136
fresh	1 medium	0.1	2	9.7	37
pear					
tinned in heavy syrup	1 cup	0.3	1	48.9	188
tinned in light syrup	1 cup	0.1	1	38.1	144
fresh	1 medium	0.7	6	25.1	98
persimmon, fresh	1 medium	0.1	3	8.4	32
pineapple pieces					
tinned, unsweetened	1 cup	0.2	1	39.2	150
fresh	1 cup	0.7	8	19.2	77
plantain, cooked, sliced	1 cup	0.3	1	48.0	179
plum					
tinned in heavy syrup	½ cup	0.1	1	30.9	119
fresh	1 medium	0.4	1	8.6	36
pomegranate, fresh	1 medium	0.5	4	26.4	104
prickly pear, fresh	1 medium	0.5	11	9.9	42
prunes, dried, cooked	½ cup	0.2	1	29.8	113
raisins & sultanas					
dark seedless	3T	0.2	2	29.7	112
golden seedless	3T	0.2	2	29.8	113
raspberries					
fresh	1 cup	0.7	10	14.2	61
frzn, sweetened	1 cup	0.4	1	65.4	256
rhubarb, diced, unsweetened	1 cup	0.2	7	5.6	26
strawberries					
fresh	1 cup	0.6	12	10.5	45
frzn, sweetened	1 cup	0.3	1	66.1	245
tangerine, fresh	1 medium	0.2	5	9.4	37
watermelon, fresh	1 cup	0.5	9	11.5	50
Fruit Juices and Nectars					
apple juice	8 fl oz / 225 ml	0.3	2	29.0	116
carrot juice	8 fl oz / 225 ml	0.4	4	22.8	97
cranberry-apple juice	8 fl oz / 225 ml	0.2	1	40.0	160
grape juice	8 fl oz / 225 ml	0.2	1	31.9	128
grapefruit juice	8 fl oz / 225 ml	0.2	2	22.1	93
lemon juice	1D	0	0	1.3	5
lime juice	1D	0	0	1.4	6

	Serving	Total fat g	% Cal from fat	Carbs in g	Cal
orange juice	8 fl oz / 225 ml	0.5	4	25.8	111
orange-grapefruit juice	8 fl oz / 225 ml	0.2	2	25.4	107
peach nectar	8 fl oz / 225 ml	0.1	1	34.7	134
pear nectar	8 fl oz / 225 ml	0	0	39.4	149
pineapple juice	8 fl oz / 225 ml	0.2	1	34.4	139
pineapple-orange juice	8 fl oz / 225 ml	0.1	1	30.6	133
prune juice	8 fl oz / 225 ml	0.1	0	44.7	181
tomato juice	8 fl oz / 225 ml	0.2	4	10.2	43
V8 juice	8 fl oz / 225 ml	0.1	2	10.2	49
Gravies, Sauces and Dips					
barbecue sauce	1D	0.3	23	2.0	12
cheese sauce, hmde	1¾ oz / 50 g	7.3	n/a	4.5	99
chilli sauce	1D	0	0	3.8	17
dip made with sour cream	2D	3.0	67	2.0	40
gravy					
from mix	3T	0.1	6	3.1	16
hmde	3T	14.0	77	8.5	164
guacamole dip	1 oz / 28 g	4.0	72	3.0	50
hollandaise sauce	3T	18.0	95	5.0	170
Ideal sauce	1D	0	n/a	2.3	9
ketchup, tomato	1D	Tr	n/a	2.6	11
mustard	1D	0.6	45	0.9	12
onion dip	2D	4.0	80	2.0	45
pesto sauce, commercial	1 oz / 28 g	14.6	85	3.0	155
sour-cream sauce	3T	7.6	53	11.4	128
soy sauce	1D	0	0	1.1	10
soy sauce, reduced sodium	1D	0	0	1.5	11
spaghetti sauce					
hmde, w/reg. beef mince	½ cup	18.7	69	11.5	243
Ragu, tomato	3½ oz / 100 g	2.8	n/a	12.1	79
spinach dip (sour cream & mayo)	2D	7.1	86	2.0	74
sweet & sour sauce	3T	0.2	2	24.0	100
tabasco sauce	1 scant t	0	0	0	1
taco sauce	1D	0	0	1.3	5
tartar sauce	1D	7.7	99	0.1	70
teriyaki sauce	1T	0	0	2.9	15
white sauce	2D	3.4	51	5.4	60
Worcestershire sauce	1D	0	0	2.0	10

Meats

(all cooked w/o added fat unless otherwise noted)

	Serving	Total fat g	% Cal from fat	Carbs in g	Cal
beef, extra lean, ≤ 5% fat (cooked)					
round, eye of, lean	3½ oz / 100 g	3.5	20	0	155
beef, lean 5–10% fat (cooked)					
flank steak, fat trimmed	3½ oz / 100 g	8.0	37	0	193
hindshank, lean	3½ oz / 100 g	9.4	41	0	207
porterhouse steak, lean	3½ oz / 100 g	10.4	42	0	225
rib steak, lean	3½ oz / 100 g	9.4	41	0	207
round or topside					
bottom, lean	3½ oz / 100 g	9.4	41	0	207
roasted	3½ oz / 100 g	7.4	35	0	189
rump, lean, pot-roasted	3½ oz / 100 g	7.0	35	0	179
topside, lean	3½ oz / 100 g	6.4	27	0	211
sirloin steak, lean	3½ oz / 100 g	8.9	40	0	201
sirloin tip, lean, roasted	3½ oz / 100 g	9.4	41	0	207
tenderloin, lean, grilled	3½ oz / 100 g	11.1	46	0	219
top sirloin, lean, grilled	3½ oz / 100 g	7.9	35	0	201
beef, regular, 11–17.4% fat (cooked)					
chuck, separable lean	3½ oz / 100 g	15.2	51	0	268
club steak, lean	3½ oz / 100 g	12.9	48	0	240
cubed steak	3½ oz / 100 g	15.4	53	0	264
hamburger, lean	3 oz / 80 g	15.7	53	0	268
rib roast, lean	3½ oz / 100 g	15.2	52	0	264
stew meat, round, raw	4 oz / 110 g	15.3	47	0	294
T-bone, lean only	3½ oz / 100 g	10.3	44	0	212
tenderloin, marbled	3½ oz / 100 g	15.2	52	0	264
beef, high fat, ≥ 17.5% fat (cooked)					
shoulder, pot-roasted	3½ oz / 100 g	26.5	67	0	354
chuck, minced	3½ oz / 100 g	23.9	66	0	327
hamburger, regular	3 oz / 80 g	19.6	62	0	286
meatballs	1 oz / 28g	5.5	63	0	78
porterhouse steak, lean & marbled	3½ oz / 100 g	19.6	62	0	286
rib steak	3½ oz / 100 g	14.7	46	0	286
rump, pot-roasted	3½ oz / 100 g	19.6	62	0	286
sirloin, grilled	3½ oz / 100 g	18.7	61	0	278
sirloin, minced	3½ oz / 100 g	26.5	67	0	354
T-bone, grilled	3½ oz / 100 g	26.5	67	0	354
beef, highest fat, ≥ 27.5% fat (cooked)					
brisket, lean & marbled	3½ oz / 100 g	30.0	73	0	367
chuck, stew meat	3½ oz / 100 g	30.0	73	0	367

	Serving	Total fat g	% Cal from fat	Carbs in g	Cal
corned, medium fat	3½ oz / 100 g	30.2	73	0	372
rib roast	3½ oz / 100 g	30.0	73	0	367
beef sausages	3½ oz / 100 g	4.9	n/a	4.3	74
lamb					
blade chop					
lean	1 chop	6.4	45	0	128
lean & marbled	3½ oz / 100 g	26.1	62	0	380
leg					
lean	3½ oz / 100 g	8.1	41	0	180
lean & marbled	3½ oz / 100 g	14.5	54	0	242
loin chop					
lean	3½ oz / 100 g	8.1	41	0	180
lean & marbled	3½ oz / 100 g	22.5	67	0	302
rib chop					
lean	3½ oz / 100 g	8.1	41	0	180
lean & marbled	3½ oz / 100 g	21.2	65	0	292
shoulder					
lean	3½ oz / 100 g	9.9	36	0	248
lean & marbled	3½ oz / 100 g	27.0	57	0	430
miscellaneous meats					
bacon substitute (turkey rashers), fried	2 rashers	2.0	n/a	1.3	60
frog legs					
cooked	4 large	0.3	3	0	73
flour-coated & fried	6 large	28.6	61	0	418
rabbit, stewed	3½ oz / 100 g	10.1	42	0	216
venison, roasted	3½ oz / 100 g	2.5	14	0	157
offal					
brains, all kinds, raw					
heart	3 oz / 80 g	7.4	63	0	106
beef, lean, braised	3½ oz / 100 g	5.6	29	0.4	175
calf, braised	3½ oz / 100 g	6.8	33	0.1	186
pig's, braised	3½ oz / 100 g	6.5	31	0.5	191
kidney					
beef, braised	3½ oz / 100 g	3.4	21	1.0	144
lamb's, fried	3½ oz / 100 g	14.0	n/a	3.9	232
liver					
beef, braised	3½ oz / 100 g	4.9	27	3.4	161
beef, fried	3½ oz / 100 g	8.0	33	7.9	217
calf, braised	3½ oz / 100 g	6.9	38	2.7	165
calf, fried	3½ oz / 100 g	11.4	42	3.9	245
tongue					

	Serving	Total fat g	% Cal from fat	Carbs in g	Cal
beef, etc., pickled	1 oz / 28 g	4.6	66	1.0	63
beef, etc., potted	1 oz / 28 g	4.7	63	0.3	6.7
beef, med. fat, braised	3½ oz / 100 g	18.6	62	0	271
pork					
bacon					
cured, grilled	1 rasher	3.1	78	0	36
cured, raw	1 rasher	13.0	93	0	126
blade					
lean	3½ oz / 100 g	9.6	39	0	219
lean, marbled	3½ oz / 100 g	18.0	56	0	290
ham					
gammon, lean	3½ oz / 100 g	5.5	34	1.5	145
gammon, lean & marbled	3½ oz / 100 g	12.9	57	0.1	203
shank, lean	3½ oz / 100 g	6.3	35	1.2	164
shank, lean & marbled	2 slices	13.8	49	0	255
tinned	3 oz / 80 g	4.6	35	0	120
ham & pork, chopped, tinned	3½ oz / 100 g	23.6	n/a	0	270
Parma	1 oz / 28 g	5.3	n/a	0	77
loin, lean, roasted	3½ oz /100 g	10.2	44	0	207
loin chop					
lean	1 chop	7.7	41	0	170
lean & fat	1 chop	22.5	64	0	314
pork pie	3⅓ oz / 100 g	27.0	n/a	24.9	376
pig's feet, pickled	1 oz / 28 g	4.6	71	<1.0	58
rib, chop, trimmed	3½ oz / 100 g	9.9	43	0	209
rib, roast, trimmed	3½ oz / 100 g	10.0	44	0	204
sausages					
beef, grilled	1 oz / 28 g	4.9	n/a	4.3	74
pork, grilled	1 oz / 28 g	6.9	n/a	3.2	89
sirloin, lean, roasted	3½ oz / 100 g	10.2	44	0	207
spareribs, roasted	6 medium	35.0	79	0	396
tenderloin, lean, roast	3½ oz / 100 g	4.8	28	0	155
top loin chop, trimmed	3½ oz / 100 g	7.7	36	0	193
top loin roast, trimmed	3½ oz / 100 g	7.5	36	0	187
processed meats					
turkey rashers, fried	2	2	n/a	1.3	60
beef jerky	1 oz /28 g	3.6	36	3.3	90
bratwurst					
pork	2-oz / 56-g link	22.0	77	1.8	256
pork & beef	2-oz / 56-g link	19.5	78	2.1	226
braunshweiger (pork liver sausage)	1 oz / 28 g	5.8	80	0.6	65

	Serving	Total fat g	% Cal from fat	Carbs in g	Cal
chicken roll	1 oz / 28 g	1.4	48	0.5	26
corned beef, jellied	1 oz / 28 g	2.9	84	0	31
ham, chopped	1 oz / 28 g	3.5	61	0.8	52
hot dog/frank					
beef	1	12.8	81	0.8	142
turkey	1	8.1	71	0.6	102
kielbasa (Polish sausage)	1 oz / 28 g	7.1	79	0.6	81
knockwurst/knackwurst	2-oz / 56-g link	18.9	81	1.2	209
liver pâté, goose	1 oz / 28 g	12.4	85	1.3	131
pepperoni	1 oz /28 g	13.0	83	1.0	140
pork & beef pepperoni	1 oz / 28 g	12.5	80	0.8	141
salami					
cooked	1 oz / 28 g	7.0	79	<1.0	80
dry/hard	1 oz / 28 g	10.0	75	0	120
sausage					
Italian	2-oz / 56-g link	17.7	82	0.4	195
Polish	1-oz / 28-g link	8.1	79	0.5	92
smoked	2 oz / 56-g link	18.0	85	1.0	190
Vienna	1 sausage	4.0	80	0.3	45
Spam	1 oz / 28 g	7.0	79	0.7	80
turkey breast	1 oz / 28 g	0.8	23	1.2	31
turkey ham	1 oz / 28 g	1.2	32	0.4	34
turkey loaf	1 oz / 28 g	2.6	54	0.4	43
turkey roll	1 oz / 28 g	4.5	56	0.7	72
veal					
blade					
lean	3½ oz / 100 g	8.4	33	0	228
lean & fat	3½ oz / 100 g	16.6	54	0	276
breast, stewed	3½ oz / 100 g	18.6	65	0	256
chuck, med. fat, braised	3½ oz / 100 g	12.8	49	0	235
flank, med. fat, stewed	3½ oz / 100 g	32.0	74	0	390
foreshank, med. fat, stewed	3½ oz / 100 g	10.4	43	0	216
loin, med. fat, broiled	3½ oz / 100 g	13.4	52	0	234
loin chop					
lean	1 chop	4.8	29	0	149
lean & fat	3½ oz / 100 g	13.3	48	0	250
rib, chop					
lean	1 chop	4.6	33	0	125
lean & fat	1 chop	18.4	63	0	264
rump, marbled, roasted	3½ oz / 100 g	11.0	44	0	225
shoulder steak					
lean	3½ oz / 100 g	4.8	24	0	180

	Serving	Total fat g	% Cal from fat	Carbs in g	Cal
lean & fat	3½ oz / 100 g	19.0	57	0	298
sirloin					
lean, roasted	3½ oz / 100 g	3.4	17	0	175
marbled, roasted	3½ oz / 100 g	6.5	32	0	181
sirloin steak					
lean	3½ oz / 100 g	6.0	26	0	204
lean & fat	3½ oz / 100 g	20.4	60	0	305

Milk and Yoghurt

	Serving	Total fat g	% Cal from fat	Carbs in g	Cal
buttermilk 1% fat	8 fl oz / 225 ml	2.2	20	11.7	99
choc. milk					
2% fat	8 fl oz / 225 ml	5.0	25	26.0	179
whole	8 fl oz / 225 ml	8.8	35	30.9	226
condensed milk, sweetened	4 fl oz / 110 ml	13.2	24	83.2	492
creamer, Coffeemate	2t	1.6	n/a	2.5	25
evaporated milk					
partly skimmed	3½ oz / 100 g	4.0	n/a	11.0	110
whole	4 fl oz / 110 ml	9.5	51	12.7	169
hot cocoa					
w/skim milk	8 fl oz / 225 ml	2.0	11	25.4	158
w/whole milk	8 fl oz / 225 ml	9.1	38	25.8	218
drinking chocolate w/whole milk	7 fl oz / 200 ml	8.4	n/a	26.4	212
Options Choc-a-Mint	7 fl oz / 200 ml	1.2	n/a	6.0	40
low-fat milk, semi-skimmed	8 fl oz / 225 ml	3.5	n/a	12.5	108
malted milk	8 fl oz / 225 ml	9.8	37	27.3	237
milkshake					
choc., thick	8 fl oz / 225 ml	14.0	23	94.0	540
vanilla, thick	8 fl oz / 225 ml	14.0	24	88.0	520
Ovaltine, w/skimmed milk	8 fl oz / 225 ml	2.6	13	29.7	182
Ski low fat yoghurt drink	8 fl oz / 225 ml	0.7	n/a	33.5	178
skimmed milk					
liquid	8 fl oz / 225 ml	0.3	n/a	11.3	77
nonfat dry powder	3T	0.2	2	15.6	109
whole milk					
liquid	8 fl oz / 225 ml	9.0	n/a	10.6	152
dry powder	3T	8.6	49	12.3	159
yoghurt					
blackcurrant, very low fat, Safeway	4½ oz / 125 g pot	0.1	n/a	6.3	45
custard style, rhubarb	4½ oz / 125 g pot	6.6	n/a	24.3	175
toffee, low fat	5¼ oz / 150 g pot	2.0	n/a	32.0	175

	Serving	Total fat g	% Cal from fat	Carbs in g	Cal
plain					
low fat	3½ oz / 100 g	0.3	n/a	7.6	54
whole milk, Safeway	5¼-oz / 150-g pot	1.7	n/a	11.0	90
Greek, with cream	3½ oz / 100g pot	10.0	n/a	3.2	128
Miscellaneous					
baking powder	1 scant t	0	0	0.7	3
bouillon cube, beef or chicken	1	0.2	20	1.1	9
choc., baking	1 oz / 28 g	15.7	95	8.0	148
cocoa, dry	4T	3.6	28	12.8	115
honey	1D	0	0	16.0	64
horseradish, prepared	1 scant t	0	0	<1.0	4
jam, all varieties	1D	0	0	12.0	48
jelly, all varieties	1D	0	0	12.0	48
marmalade	1D	0	0	12.0	50
molasses	1D	0	0	14.0	60
olives					
black	2 large	3.5	97	1.0	36
Greek	3 medium	10.2	96	2.5	96
green	2 medium	1.0	90	0.6	10
pickle/relish					
sweet	1D	0.1	5	5.3	19
mango chutney	2t	Tr	n/a	5.3	22
pickles					
bread & butter	4 slices	0.1	4	5.4	22
dill or sour	1 large	0.1	8	2.7	12
Kosher	1 oz / 28 g	0.1	22	0.6	4
sweet	1 oz / 28 g	0.4	7	11.6	50
salt	1 scant t	0	0	0	0
spices/seasonings	1 scant t	0.2	36	1.4	5
sugar, all varieties	1D	0	0	11.9	46
sugar substitutes	1 packet	0	0	<1.0	4
syrup, all varieties	1D	0	0	15.0	60
vinegar	1D	0	0	0.9	2
yeast	1D	0	0	3.0	20
Nuts and Seeds					
almond paste/marzipan	1D	39	55	6.2	64
almonds	12–15	9.3	81	3.5	104
Brazil nuts	4 medium	9.4	91	1.8	93
cashews, roasted	6–8	7.0	74	4.0	85
chestnuts, fresh	3 small	0.6	9	12.9	60
coconut, dried, shredded	4T	11.0	64	14.8	155

	Serving	Total fat g	% Cal from fat	Carbs in g	Cal
hazelnuts (filberts)	10–12	9.4	80	3.3	106
macadamia nuts, roasted	5 medium	10.9	96	1.9	102
mixed nuts					
w/peanuts	8–12	10.0	83	4.1	109
w/o peanuts	2D	10.1	83	3.9	110
peanut butter, creamy or chunky	1D	8.0	76	3.5	94
peanuts					
chopped	2D	7.0	62	6.8	102
honey roasted	2D	13.0	78	4.0	150
in shell	1 cup	17.7	76	5.2	209
pecans	2D	9.2	89	3.2	93
pine nuts (pignolia)	2D	8.6	88	2.4	88
pistachios	2D	7.7	75	3.9	92
poppy seeds	1D	3.9	75	2.1	47
pumpkin seeds	2D	7.9	76	3.1	93
sesame seeds	2D	9.0	78	4.2	104
sunflower seeds	2D	9.5	82	3.4	104
trail mix w/seeds, nuts, carob	2D	6.0	51	11.0	105
walnuts	2D	8.1	84	11.7	86

Pasta, Noodles and Rice
(all measurements after cooking unless otherwise noted)

	Serving	Total fat g	% Cal from fat	Carbs in g	Cal
macaroni					
semolina	1 cup	0.9	4	0.4	197
whole wheat	1 cup	0.8	4	37.2	174
noodles					
cellophane, fried	1 cup	4.2	27	24.8	141
chow mein, tinned	½ cup	8.0	48	16.0	150
egg	1 cup	2.4	10	39.7	212
manicotti	1 cup	0.4	3	25.8	129
ramen, all varieties	1 cup	8.0	38	26.0	190
rice	1 cup	0.3	2	30.4	140
romanoff	1 cup	22.0	41	56.0	480
rice					
brown	½ cup	0.9	7	22.4	108
fried	½ cup	5.0	28	25.0	160
long grain & wild	½ cup	2.1	16	22.5	120
pilaf	½ cup	6.0	28	30.0	190
Spanish style	½ cup	0.4	3	25.7	120
white	½ cup	0.2	1	29.3	133
spaghetti, enriched	1 cup	0.9	4	39.7	197
taco shells	2 shells	5.1	n/a	13.7	47

	Serving	Total fat g	% Cal from fat	Carbs in g	Cal
Poultry					
chicken					
breast					
w/skin, fried	½ breast	8.7	36	1.6	218
w/o skin, fried	½ breast	4.1	23	0.4	161
w/skin, roasted	½ breast	7.6	35	0	193
w/o skin, roasted	½ breast	3.1	20	0	142
fried					
w/skin, batter dipped	3½ oz / 100 g	17.4	54	9.4	289
w/o skin	3½ oz / 100 g	11.6	44	2.6	239
giblets, fried	3½ oz / 100 g	13.5	44	4.4	277
gizzard, simmered	3½ oz / 100 g	4.8	27	1.0	157
heart, simmered	3½ oz / 100 g	7.9	38	0.1	185
leg					
w/skin, fried	1 leg	16.2	51	2.8	285
w/skin, roasted	1 leg	15.4	52	0	265
w/o skin, roasted	1 leg	8.1	39	0	187
liver, simmered	3½ oz / 100 g	5.5	31	0.9	157
roasted					
w/skin	3½ oz / 100 g	13.6	51	0	239
w/o skin	3½ oz / 100 g	7.4	35	0	190
roll, light meat	3½ oz / 100 g	7.4	42	2.5	159
stewers/older birds					
w/skin	3½ oz / 100 g	18.9	60	0	285
w/o skin	3½ oz / 100 g	11.9	45	0	237
thigh					
w/skin, fried	1 thigh	9.3	52	2.0	162
w/skin, roasted	1 thigh	9.6	0	56	153
w/o skin, roasted	1 thigh	5.7	47	0	109
wing					
w/skin, fried	1 wing	7.1	62	0.8	103
w/o skin, roasted	1 wing	6.6	60	0	99
duck					
w/skin, roasted	3½ oz / 100 g	28.4	76	0	337
w/o skin, roasted	3½ oz / 100 g	11.2	50	0	201
turkey					
breast					
barbecued	3½ oz / 100 g	3.2	24	3.7	118
oven roasted	3½ oz / 100 g	3.2	26	1.7	111
smoked	3½ oz / 100 g	3.7	28	0.9	118

	Serving	Total fat g	% Cal from fat	Carbs in g	Cal
dark meat					
w/skin, roasted	3½ oz / 100 g	11.5	47	0	221
w/o skin, roasted	3½ oz / 100 g	7.2	35	0	187
ground	3½ oz / 100 g	13.3	55	0	219
ham, cured	3½ oz / 100 g	5.1	36	0.4	128
light meat					
w/skin, roasted	3½ oz / 100 g	9.7	42	0	208
w/o skin, roasted	3½ oz / 100 g	5.0	26	0	170
loaf, breast meat	3½ oz / 100 g	1.6	13	0	110
patties, breaded/fried	1 patty	16.9	57	14.8	266
rashers, fried	3½ oz / 100 g	4	n/a	2.5	120
roll, light meat	3½ oz / 100 g	7.2	44	0.5	147
sausage, cooked	1 oz / 28 g	3.6	57	0.1	57
Salad Dressings					
blue cheese					
low cal	1D	1.9	63	1.7	27
regular	1D	8.0	94	1.1	77
Caesar	1T	8.0	94	0.8	76
French					
creamy	1D	6.9	89	1.9	70
fat free	1D	0	0	3.0	18
low cal	1D	0.9	37	3.5	22
regular	1D	6.4	86	2.7	67
honey mustard	1D	6.6	67	7.1	89
Italian					
creamy	1D	5.5	92	1.4	54
low cal	1D	1.5	84	0.7	16
mayonnaise type					
low cal	1D	1.8	85	0.7	19
regular	1D	4.9	77	3.5	57
oil & vinegar	1D	7.5	98	0.4	69
Russian					
low cal	1D	0.7	26	4.5	24
regular	1D	7.8	92	1.6	76
Salad creams					
Heinz regular	1D	2.9	n/a	2.4	36
Heinz light	1D	2.3	n/a	1.3	26
Weight Watchers	1D	6.4	n/a	1.8	11
sesame seed	1D	6.9	91	1.3	68
sweet & sour	1D	0.9	28	5.2	29

	Serving	Total fat g	% Cal from fat	Carbs in g	Cal
Thousand Island					
fat free	1D	0	0	5.0	20
low cal	1D	1.6	60	2.5	24
regular	1D	5.6	85	2.4	59
Snack Foods					
Cheddars, McVities	5 biscuits	6.5	n/a	10.0	105
Cheese Puff balls	1 oz / 28 g	10.6	59	16.0	161
cheese straws	4 pieces	7.2	59	8.3	109
party mix (cereal, pretzels, nuts)	1 cup	23.0	66	22.3	312
popcorn					
air popped	1 cup	0.3	8	6.3	31
caramel	1 cup	4.5	27	27.9	152
popped w/oil	1 cup	3.1	51	6.2	55
potato crisps					
individually	10 crisps	8.0	64	9.1	113
by weight	1 oz / 28 g	9.8	58	15.0	152
barbecue flavour	1 oz / 28 g	9.2	59	15.0	139
light, Pringles	1 oz / 28 g	8.0	48	17.0	150
regular, Pringles	1 oz / 28 g	12.0	63	12.0	170
potato rings, St Michaels					
reduced fat	1 oz / 28 g	4.3	n/a	18.4	120
potato sticks	1 oz / 28 g	9.8	59	15.1	148
pretzels	1 oz / 28 g	1.0	8	22.5	108
rice cakes	1	0	10	7.0	35
tortilla chips					
regular	1 oz / 28 g	7.0	45	18.0	140
no oil, baked	1 oz / 28 g	1.5	12	24.0	110
Tostitos	1 oz / 28 g	8.0	48	17.0	150
Soups					
asparagus					
cream of, w/milk	8 fl oz / 225 ml	8.2	46	16.4	161
cream of, w/water	8 fl oz / 225 ml	4.1	42	10.4	87
bean					
w/bacon	8 fl oz / 225 ml	5.9	31	22.8	173
w/franks	8 fl oz / 225 ml	7.0	34	22.0	187
w/ham	8 fl oz / 225 ml	8.5	33	27.1	231
w/o meat	8 fl oz / 225 ml	1.0	7	24.7	130
beef					
clear broth	8 fl oz / 225 ml	0.1	6	0.6	14
chunky	8 fl oz / 225 ml	5.1	27	19.6	171

	Serving	Total fat g	% Cal from fat	Carbs in g	Cal
beef barley	8 fl oz / 225 ml	1.0	15	10.0	59
broccoli, creamy, w/water	8 fl oz / 225 ml	2.8	37	9.3	69
chicken					
chunky	8 fl oz / 225 ml	6.0	32	19.0	170
cream of, w/milk	8 fl oz / 225 ml	11.5	42	15.0	191
cream of, w/water	8 fl oz / 225 ml	7.4	57	9.3	116
chicken & wild rice	8 fl oz / 225 ml	2.0	23	12.4	80
chicken gumbo	8 fl oz / 225 ml	1.4	23	8.4	56
chicken mushroom	8 fl oz / 225 ml	9.2	63	9.3	132
chicken noodle					
chunky	8 fl oz / 225 ml	5.2	31	14.9	149
w/water	8 fl oz / 225 ml	2.5	30	9.4	75
chicken vegetable					
chunky	8 fl oz / 225 ml	4.8	26	18.9	167
w/water	8 fl oz / 225 ml	2.8	34	8.6	74
chicken w/rice					
chunky	8 fl oz / 225 ml	3.2	23	13.0	127
w/water	8 fl oz / 225 ml	1.9	29	7.2	60
consommé w/gelatin	8 fl oz / 225 ml	0	0	1.8	29
crab	8 fl oz / 225 ml	1.5	18	10.3	76
dehydrated					
asparagus, cream of	8 fl oz / 225 ml	1.7	26	9.0	59
bean w/bacon	8 fl oz / 225 ml	2.2	19	16.4	105
beef broth cube	1 cube	0.5	32	1.4	14
beef noodle	8 fl oz / 225 ml	0.7	15	1.9	41
cauliflower	8 fl oz / 225 ml	1.7	23	10.7	68
chicken, cream of	8 fl oz / 225 ml	5.3	45	13.4	107
chicken broth cube	1 cube	0.2	20	1.1	9
chicken noodle	8 fl oz / 225 ml	1.2	20	7.4	53
chicken rice	8 fl oz / 225 ml	1.4	21	9.3	60
Cup a Soup					
asparagus	1 pkg	6.5	n/a	17.1	127
chicken	1 pkg	5.6	n/a	11.6	100
tomato	1 pkg	1.9	n/a	15.7	78
minestrone	8 fl oz / 225 ml	1.7	19	11.9	79
mushroom	8 fl oz / 225 ml	4.9	46	11.1	96
onion					
dry mix	1 pkg	2.3	18	20.9	115
prepared	8 fl oz / 225 ml	0.5	17	4.7	27
Slim a soup					
broccoli & cauliflower	pkg	2.4	n/a	8.4	59
chicken noodle & veg	pkg	1.0	n/a	8.7	55

	Serving	Total fat g	% Cal from fat	Carbs in g	Cal
minestrone	pkg	0.6	n/a	10.2	57
tomato	8 fl oz / 225 ml	2.4	21	19.4	102
vegetable beef	8 fl oz / 225 ml	1.1	19	8.0	53
gazpacho w/o fat	8 fl oz / 225 ml	0.2	4	8.8	41
Heinz big soup					
chicken & ham	7 oz / 200 g	2.3	n/a	13.7	93
hmde or restaurant style					
celery, cream of, w/whole milk	8 fl oz / 225 ml	9.7	53	14.5	164
clear chicken broth	8 fl oz / 225 ml	1.4	33	6.0	38
corn chowder, traditional	8 fl oz / 225 ml	15.0	45	36.0	298
gazpacho, traditional	8 fl oz / 225 ml	7.0	63	8.7	100
onion, French, w/o cheese	8 fl oz / 225 ml	5.8	46	14.4	114
oyster stew, w/whole milk	8 fl oz / 225 ml	8.0	54	9.8	134
lentil	8 fl oz / 225 ml	2.1	10	29.9	181
minestrone					
chunky	8 fl oz / 225 ml	2.8	20	20.7	127
w/water	8 fl oz / 225 ml	2.5	27	11.2	83
mushroom, cream of					
condensed	1 tin	23.1	66	22.6	313
w/milk	8 fl oz / 225 ml	13.6	60	15.0	203
w/water	8 fl oz / 225 ml	9.0	63	9.3	129
onion	8 fl oz / 225 ml	1.7	27	8.2	57
oyster stew, w/water	8 fl oz / 225 ml	3.8	58	4.1	59
pea					
green, w/water	8 fl oz / 225 ml	2.9	16	26.5	164
split	8 fl oz / 225 ml	0.8	5	23.6	143
split w/ham	8 fl oz / 225 ml	4.4	21	28.0	189
potato, cream of, w/milk	8 fl oz / 225 ml	6.5	39	17.2	148
shrimp, cream of, w/milk	8 fl oz / 225 ml	9.3	51	13.9	165
tomato					
w/milk	8 fl oz / 225 ml	6.0	34	22.3	160
w/water	8 fl oz / 225 ml	1.9	20	16.6	86
tomato beef w/noodle	8 fl oz / 225 ml	4.3	28	21.2	140
tomato bisque, w/milk	8 fl oz / 225 ml	6.6	30	29.4	198
tomato rice	8 fl oz / 225 ml	2.7	20	21.9	120
turkey, chunky	8 fl oz / 225 ml	5.1	36	13.7	128
turkey, noodle	8 fl oz / 225 ml	2.0	26	8.6	69
turkey, vegetable	8 fl oz / 225 ml	3.0	36	8.6	74
vegetable, chunky	8 fl oz / 225 ml	3.7	27	19.0	122
vegetable w/beef, chunky	8 fl oz / 225 ml	3.7	24	14.1	141
vegetable, w/beef broth	8 fl oz / 225 ml	1.9	22	10.2	79
vegetable w/out meat	8 fl oz / 225 ml	1.6	24	9.0	59

	Serving	Total fat g	% Cal from fat	Carbs in g	Cal
vegetarian vegetable	8 fl oz / 225 ml	1.2	15	13.3	73
Weight Watchers					
chicken noodle	10-oz / 295-g can	0.6	n/a	9.2	52
mushroom	10-oz / 295-g can	1.9	n/a	10.4	70
Sweets and Chocolate Bars					
boiled	6 pieces	0	n/a	27.8	106
butterscotch	6 pieces	1.0	8	26.9	113
candied fruit					
apricot	1 oz / 28 g	0.1	1	24.2	94
cherry	1 oz / 28 g	0.1	1	24.6	96
citrus peel	1 oz / 28 g	0.1	1	22.9	90
figs	1 oz / 28 g	0.1	1	20.6	84
chewing gum	1 piece	0	0	2.0	10
chocolate bar					
Crunchie	snack size	4.4	n/a	16.7	105
	large bar	8.0	n/a	30.5	195
Kit Kat	1.13 oz / 32 g	9.2	49	19.8	169
Mars	1.7 oz / 48 g	11.0	41	30.0	240
Milky Way	1 oz / 28 g	5.0	35	20.0	130
Snickers	1 oz / 28 g	6.5	43	16.5	135
Twix	1 oz / 28 g	6.7	44	17.8	136
caramels					
plain or choc. w/nuts	1 oz / 28 g	4.6	34	20.0	121
plain or choc. w/o nuts	1 oz / 28 g	3.0	25	20.0	110
choc. chips					
milk choc.	3T	10.5	42	28.5	225
semisweet	3T	13.0	53	31.0	220
choc.-covered cherries	1 oz / 28 g	2.0	16	21.0	110
choc.-covered cream centre	1 oz / 28 g	3.7	28	22.3	120
choc.-covered mint	1 small	1.2	24	8.9	45
choc.-covered peanuts	1 oz / 28 g	9.0	51	14.0	160
choc.-covered raisins	1 oz / 28 g	5.0	35	20.0	130
fudge					
choc.	1 oz / 28 g	2.3	19	22.5	108
choc. w/nuts	1 oz / 28 g	4.6	34	20.6	121
gumdrops	10 small	0	0	34.6	135
jelly beans	1 oz / 28 g	0	0	26.0	100
liquorice	1 oz / 28 g	1.0	9	23.0	100
Life Savers	5 pieces	0	0	10.0	40
M&M's					
choc. only	1 oz / 28 g	6.0	39	20.0	140

	Serving	Total fat g	% Cal from fat	Carbs in g	Cal
peanut	1 oz / 28 g	7.0	14	17.0	150
malted-milk balls	1 oz / 28 g	5.0	35	21.0	130
marshmallow	1 large	0	0	6.0	25
mints	5 pieces	0	0	10.0	40
Opal Fruits	1¾ oz / 45 g pack	3.4	n/a	38.3	185
peanut brittle	1 oz / 28 g	5.4	38	19.7	128
peppermints	½ oz / 14 g	0.1	n/a	14.3	55
praline	1 oz / 28 g	6.9	49	1.7	128
sour balls	1 oz / 28 g	0	0	27.0	110
sugar coated almonds	1 oz / 28 g	2.0	15	23.0	120
toffees	1 oz / 28 g	5.0	n/a	20.3	123
yoghurt-covered peanuts	½ cup	25.0	50	47.0	450

Vegetables

	Serving	Total fat g	% Cal from fat	Carbs in g	Cal
alfalfa bean sprouts, raw	½ cup	0.1	18	0.7	5
artichoke, boiled	1 medium	0.2	3	13.4	53
artichoke hearts, boiled	½ cup	0.1	2	8.7	37
asparagus, cooked	½ cup	0.3	12	3.8	22
aubergine, cooked	½ cup	0.1	7	3.2	13
avocado					
California	1 (6 oz / 175 g)	30.0	88	12.0	306
Florida	1 (11 oz / 325 g)	27.0	72	27.1	339
bamboo shoots, raw	½ cup	0.2	9	4.0	21
beans					
all types, cooked w/o fat	½ cup	0.4	3	16.7	143
baked, brown sugar & molasses	½ cup	1.5	10	24.2	132
baked, vegetarian	½ cup	0.6	5	26.1	118
Heinz tinned with tomato sauce	3¾ oz / 105 g	0.2	n/a	14.3	158
beetroot, pickled	½ cup	0.1	1	18.6	75
black-eyed beans, cooked	½ cup	0.6	5	17.3	100
broccoli					
cooked	½ cup	0.3	12	4.0	22
frzn, chopped, cooked	½ cup	0.1	4	4.9	25
in butter sauce	½ cup	2.0	45	5.9	40
w/cheese sauce	½ cup	6.2	48	11.6	116
raw	½ cup	0.2	15	2.3	12
brussels sprouts, cooked	½ cup	0.4	12	6.8	30
butter beans, tinned	½ cup	0.4	5	15.9	76
cabbage					
Chinese, raw	1 cup	0.2	18	1.6	10
green, cooked	½ cup	0.1	6	3.6	16
red, raw, shredded	½ cup	0.1	9	2.1	10

	Serving	Total fat g	% Cal from fat	Carbs in g	Cal
carrot					
cooked	½ cup	0.1	3	8.2	35
raw	1 cup	0.1	3	7.3	31
cauliflower					
cooked	1 cup	0.2	6	5.8	30
w/cheese sauce	½ cup	6.1	48	11.7	114
raw	1 cup	0.1	7	2.5	12
celery					
cooked	½ cup	0.1	7	3.0	13
raw	1 stalk	0.1	15	1.5	6
chard, cooked	½ cup	0.1	5	3.6	18
chickpeas, cooked	½ cup	2.1	14	22.5	135
chillies, green	¼ cup	0	0	2.0	10
Chinese-style vegetables, frzn	½ cup	4.0	49	7.4	74
chives, raw, chopped	1T	0	0	0.1	1
corn					
corn on the cob	1 medium	1.0	7	28.7	120
cream style, tinned	½ cup	0.5	5	23.2	93
frzn, cooked	½ cup	0.1	1	16.8	67
frzn w/butter sauce	½ cup	2.2	18	21.8	110
whole kernel, cooked	½ cup	1.1	11	20.6	89
courgette, cooked	½ cup	0.1	6	3.5	14
cucumber					
w/skin	½ medium	0.2	9	4.4	20
w/o skin, sliced	½ cup	0.1	13	1.5	7
dandelion greens, cooked	½ cup	0.3	16	3.3	17
endive	1 cup	0.2	23	1.6	8
green beans					
French, cooked	½ cup	0.2	7	5.9	26
runner, cooked	½ cup	0.2	8	4.9	22
kale, cooked	½ cup	0.3	13	3.7	21
kidney beans, red, cooked	½ cup	0.5	4	20.2	112
leeks, chopped, raw	¼ cup	0.1	6	3.7	16
lentils, cooked	½ cup	0.4	3	19.9	116
lettuce	1 cup	0.2	18	2.0	10
lima beans, cooked	½ cup	0.4	3	19.7	108
marrow, cooked	3½ oz / 100 g	Tr	n/a	1.4	7
miso (soybean product)	½ cup	8.4	27	38.6	284
mushrooms					
tinned	½ cup	0.2	9	3.9	19
fried/sautéed	4 medium	7.4	85	1.4	78
raw	½ cup	0.2	20	1.6	9

	Serving	Total fat g	% Cal from fat	Carbs in g	Cal
mustard greens, cooked	½ cup	0.2	16	1.5	11
okra, cooked	½ cup	0.1	4	5.8	25
onions, chopped, raw	½ cup	0.1	3	6.9	30
parsley, chopped, raw	¼ cup	0.1	18	0.9	5
parsnips, cooked	½ cup	0.2	3	15.2	63
peas, green, cooked	½ cup	0.2	3	12.5	67
pepper, bell, chopped, raw	½ cup	0.1	7	3.2	13
pimientos, tinned	1 oz / 28 g	0	0	2.0	10
plantain, cooked	1 cup	0.7	8	19.2	77
potato					
au gratin, hmde	½ cup	9.3	52	13.7	160
baked w/skin	1 medium	0.2	1	51.0	220
boiled w/o skin	½ cup	0.1	1	27.0	116
french fries					
frzn	10 pieces	4.4	36	17.0	111
hmde	10 pieces	8.3	47	20.0	158
hash browns	½ cup	10.9	60	16.6	163
mashed					
from flakes, w/milk & marg.	½ cup	6.0	41	17.0	130
hmde w/milk & marg.	½ cup	4.4	36	17.5	111
potato pancakes	1 cake	12.6	48	26.4	237
potato puffs, frzn, prep. w/oil	½ cup	6.7	44	18.9	138
scalloped					
hmde	½ cup	4.5	39	132	105
w/cheese	½ cup	9.7	49	13.4	177
pumpkin, tinned	½ cup	0.3	6	9.9	41
radish, raw	10	0.2	26	1.6	7
rhubarb, raw	1 cup	0.2	6	7.0	29
sauerkraut, tinned	½ cup	0.2	8	5.1	22
soybeans, mature, cooked	½ cup	7.7	47	8.6	149
spinach					
cooked	½ cup	0.2	9	3.4	21
creamed	½ cup	5.1	58	6.8	79
raw	1 cup	0.2	15	2.0	12
spring greens, cooked	½ cup	0.1	5	3.9	17
spring onions, raw	5 medium	0.2	3	13.0	60
squash					
acorn					
baked	½ cup	0.1	2	14.9	57
mashed w/o fat	½ cup	0.1	2	10.7	41
butternut, cooked	½ cup	0.1	2	10.7	41

	Serving	Total fat g	% Cal from fat	Carbs in g	Cal
summer					
cooked	½ cup	0.3	15	3.9	18
raw, slice	½ cup	0.1	7	2.8	13
winter, cooked	½ cup	0.6	14	8.9	39
sweet potato					
baked	1 small	0.1	1	27.7	118
candied	½ cup	3.4	21	29.3	144
mashed w/o fat	½ cup	0.5	3	39.8	172
tempeh (soybean product)	½ cup	6.4	35	14.1	165
tofu (soybean curd), raw, firm	4 oz / 110 g	4.0	40	4.0	90
tomato					
raw	1 medium	0.4	14	5.7	26
stewed	½ cup	0.2	5	8.3	34
tomato paste, tinned	½ cup	1.2	10	24.7	110
turnip greens, cooked	½ cup	0.2	12	3.1	15
turnips, cooked	½ cup	0.1	6	3.8	14
water chestnuts, tinned, sliced	½ cup	0	0	8.7	35
watercress, raw	½ cup	0	0	0.2	2
wax beans, canned	½ cup	0.2	7	4.5	25
Vegetable Salads					
carrot-raisin salad	½ cup	5.8	34	27.9	153
chef salad w/o dressing	1 cup	4.2	58	2.5	65
coleslaw					
w/mayo-type dressing	½ cup	10.5	68	11.1	140
w/vinaigrette	½ cup	3.0	35	10.7	78
macaroni salad w/mayo	½ cup	12.8	58	20.8	200
potato salad					
German style	½ cup	3.0	23	23.0	120
w/mayo dressing	½ cup	10.3	52	14.0	179
salad bar items					
alfalfa sprouts	2D	0	0	0.5	2
bacon bits	1D	1.0	43	0	21
beets, pickled	2D	0	0	4.5	18
broccoli, raw	2D	0	0	0.6	3
carrots, raw	2D	0	0	0.3	6
cheese, shredded	2D	4.6	74	0.2	56
chickpeas	2D	0.3	8	6.8	36
cottage cheese	½ cup	5.1	39	3.0	116
croutons	½ oz / 14 g	2.6	38	8.0	62
cucumber	2D	0	0	0.4	2
eggs, cooked, chopped	2D	1.9	63	0.2	27

	Serving	Total fat g	% Cal from fat	Carbs in g	Cal
lettuce	½ cup	0	0	0.8	4
mushrooms, raw	2D	0	0	0.3	2
onion, raw	2D	0.1	12	1.5	7
pepper, green, raw	2D	0	0	0.7	3
potato salad	½ cup	10.3	52	14.0	179
tomato, raw	2 slices	0	0	0.4	2
tabbouli salad	½ cup	9.5	49	18.0	173
taco salad w/taco sauce	1 cup	15.3	61	13.2	226
three-bean salad	½ cup	8.2	51	15.5	145
Waldorf salad w/mayo	½ cup	12.7	73	9.1	157

Appendix D

LOCAL HELPLINES

Two British organizations which will give information and advice on smoking cessation are:

Action on Smoking and Health (ASH)
109 Gloucester Place
London W1H 3PH
Tel: 0(1)71 935 3519
Fax: 0(1)71 935 3463

Quit
102 Gloucester Place
London W1H 3DA
Tel: 0(1)71 487 3000
Or: (Scotland)   0800 848484
         (N. Ireland)   0(1)232 663281
         (Wales)   0(1)222 641888

Index